T0167809

A SHORT HISTORY

of the WORLD in 50 ANIMALS

Also by Dr Jacob F. Field

We Shall Fight on the Beaches
One Bloody Thing After Another
D–Day in Numbers
The Eccentric Mr Churchill
The History of Europe in Bite–sized Chunks
A Short History of the World in 50 Places

A SHORT HISTORY

of the

WORLD *in*

50 ANIMALS

Dr Jacob F. Field

Michael O'Mara Books Limited

For my incredible and amazing aunts, uncles and cousins around the world, thank you for the love and support over the years.

First published in Great Britain in 2021 by
Michael O'Mara Books Limited
9 Lion Yard
Tremadoc Road
London SW4 7NQ

A CIP catalogue record for this book is available from the British Library.

Papers used by Michael O'Mara Books Limited are natural, recyclable products made from wood grown in sustainable forests. The manufacturing processes conform to the environmental regulations of the country of origin.

ISBN: 978-1-78929-295-4 in hardback print format
ISBN: 978-1-78929-341-8 in trade paperback format
ISBN: 978-1-78929-296-1 in ebook format

1 2 3 4 5 6 7 8 9 10

Designed and typeset by Claire Cater
Illustrations by Aubrey Smith
Printed and bound by CPI Group (UK) Ltd, Croydon, CR0 4YY
www.mombooks.com

CONTENTS

.·⫸ ⫷·.

INTRODUCTION

.·⇒⟫ ⟪⇐·.

This book is a history of the world, from the time of the earliest life forms to the twenty-first century, told through the stories of fifty different animals, and their impact and significance. The animals considered range from microscopic to massive, from extinct to flourishing, from domesticated to wild, and are drawn from every corner of the Earth.

A Short History of the World in 50 Animals begins with an exploration of some of the most important early animals, including the origins of how water-based animals began to evolve to adapt to life on land, as well as the dinosaurs, who roamed the planet for millions of years. Although the majority of dinosaurs became extinct, a group of them survived as birds, which continue to flourish today. This chapter examines the debates that arose about how life on Earth developed, and how the Galápagos finches helped inspire the theory of evolution. This had huge implications for how humans viewed Creation, including their evolutionary link to the great apes. Chapter two details how animals have been used to help humans live and prosper, as well as fight each other. It includes some of the most important domesticated animals – from the very first, the dog, to other important agricultural species like horses, chickens, pigs and llamas. It also details how geese saved ancient Rome from total destruction in 390 BC and how the emu became the focus of a military campaign but ultimately emerged victorious. The third chapter shows the huge symbolic role animals play in mythology, religion and culture. While some are largely maligned, like the tricky red fox, the mischievous monkey and the destructive bat, others, like the Eurasian brown bear, are venerated as protective totems, and the dove is a symbol of love and purity. Other animals are linked to great empires and political power, such as the grey wolf, the lion and the eagle. Chapter four considers how animals have contributed to science, health and medicine. It includes the animals that, in absolute terms, have been the most deadly to humans – the flea and mosquito – as well as those that have helped treat us, like the leech and the guinea pig. Animals have also been the subject of intense study, particularly related to their intelligence, as the stories of Clever Hans the horse and David Greybeard the chimpanzee show. The final chapter provides examples of how animals have been used in trade and industry, going back to some of the first to be domesticated, such as the cow. It then looks at how two animals, the silkworm and the dromedary camel, have helped to stimulate and facilitate long-distance trade for centuries. Finally, it examines how humans have exploited marine creatures, in particular the largest animal to have ever lived, the blue whale.

There is much to be learned from how animals have shaped, and contributed to, human history. Whether they are individual creatures, large families of animals or a particular species, they have all had an important impact, be it cultural, economic, scientific, military or political.

1

EARLY SPECIES

TIKTAALIK

. . . .

One of the most significant 'events' in evolutionary history was when fish began to move out of the water to live on land, and their fins developed into limbs. This marked the origin of the tetrapods, a huge group of four-limbed animals that includes amphibians, reptiles, birds and mammals. Once on land, animal life became more diverse because of the wider range of living conditions, as well as the challenges of adapting to breathing, breeding and eating outside of the water. As a result, there are ten times more species on land than in the oceans.

This monumental shift happened during the Devonian Period, between 419 and 359 million years ago. In 2010, fossilized footprints of four-legged vertebrates dating to around 395 million years ago were found in the Holy Cross Mountains in south-eastern Poland. This is the earliest known evidence of a tetrapod. No fossil of the animal itself has been located. The oldest animal that shows how water-based animals may have made the transition to the land is a prehistoric fish called the *Tiktaalik*.

During the Devonian Period, oceans covered 85 per cent of the Earth. These waters were teeming with life forms, and species battled to survive. Before *Tiktaalik* was discovered, palaeontologists had theorized that during the mid- to late Devonian Period many animals were shifting towards being able to live in shallow waters, marshes and riverbeds. They would have had features common to both water- and land-based animals. As such, researchers looked for fossils of these animals in rocks that were about this age that had been part of a river delta. One such concentration was on Ellesmere Island, located in the most northerly part of Canada, within the Arctic Circle. During the Devonian Period, the island was part of a land mass called Laurasia, which was the northern part of the supercontinent Pangaea. Laurasia was made up of North America, Greenland and Europe. As the equator ran through Laurasia at this time, the conditions there were warm and tropical. This meant the coastal inlets and rivers of the continent would have been home to an abundance of potential food sources. Living closer to the water also allowed animals to more easily regulate their body temperature by basking in the sun.

In 2004, after four years of searching on Ellesmere Island, a research team found fossils of an animal 375 million years old whose anatomy was a mixture of a fish and a tetrapod. They named the genus (category of living organisms above a species) *Tiktaalik*, which means 'large, freshwater fish' in the language of the Nunavut people who are indigenous to the area. The species they found, named *Tiktaalik roseae*, is not a direct ancestor of modern tetrapods, but nonetheless the *Tiktaalik* is the earliest known example of how aquatic life forms might have made the transition to terrestrial living.

Analysis of the fossils showed that the *Tiktaalik* was up to 2.7 metres (about 9 feet) in length. Like fish, it had scales and gills. It was also ray-finned (meaning its fins were webs of skin supported by small bones), enabling it to paddle through the water more effectively. It also had features more common to tetrapods such as thick ribs and lungs. In addition, the *Tiktaalik* had nostril-like features called spiracles that perhaps developed into the middle ear in similar species. The *Tiktaalik*'s fins had strong interior bones, which was how tetrapods may have developed limbs. This meant *Tiktaalik* was able to prop the front of its body up in shallow waters. It could also snap up prey, thanks to its ability to turn its crocodile-like head laterally without moving its body – something fish cannot do. Later analysis of the fossil record showed that the *Tiktaalik* had a robust hip and pelvis, which gave its rear limbs a higher degree of power, something more common to tetrapods than fish. This meant that it was probably able to scramble across mudflats.

On the land were a range of life forms that had already been established on the surface for millions of years. Some plants had already made the transition, as had other animal groups such as insects, arachnids and molluscs. These would all have been a potentially rich food source for a water-based animal to exploit, should it be able to adapt to land. Ultimately, the *Tiktaalik* would have faced less competition on land than it did in the water, where it was rivalled by larger species of fish, some of which measured over 6 metres (about 20 feet) in length. It is unknown where the evolutionary path of the *Tiktaalik* ultimately ended, as it has no living descendent species. The *Tiktaalik* may never have fully adapted to living on land but it showed how a huge range of animal species can trace their distant origins to the ocean.

DICKINSONIA

Living 558 million years ago, the oldest known family of animals are *Dickinsonia* – thin, ribbed, oval-shaped life forms that could grow to about 1.4 metres (nearly 5 feet) long. Once thought to perhaps be a fungus, the discovery of cholesterol in its fossils showed it digested food, proving it was instead an animal.

THE DINOSAURS

....

Few animal groups attract as much attention, study and fascination as the dinosaurs. These reptiles spread across every corner of the Earth during the Mesozoic Era, which began 252 million years ago. However, 66 million years ago the vast majority of the dinosaurs became extinct in a cataclysmic event that transformed animal life on this planet.

Humans have been finding dinosaur bones and fossils since at least the seventh century BC. At first, no one knew exactly what they were. It is possible some ancient peoples mistook them for mythical creatures like the griffin, and even as late as the seventeenth century AD scholars believed them to be the remains of a race of gigantic humans. Things began to change in the early nineteenth century, when an increasing number of dinosaur remains had been dug up across Europe and North America. This group of animals did not have a name until the English biologist Sir Richard Owen (1804–92) formally proposed dinosaur, which meant 'Terrible Reptile', in 1842. Owen had viewed specimens of dinosaurs unearthed in southern England. He had realized they were their own distinct group because they differed from contemporary reptiles, notably because they held their limbs perpendicularly under their bodies rather than sprawled to the side. Owen's classification began to be widely used; he went on to advise the Great Exhibition of 1851, act as a tutor to the royal family and was central to the founding of the Natural History Museum. During the second half of the nineteenth century, there was a wave of interest in dinosaur studies, leading to the 'Bone Wars', where the rival American scholars Othniel Charles Marsh (1831–99) and Edward Drinker Cope (1840–97) battled each other to dig up and identify new species. They would eventually discover 142 between them.

There are now over 1,000 recognized species of dinosaur, which have been discovered on every continent (including

Antarctica). About fifty new species of dinosaur are being discovered every year, largely because of a higher number of digs in the deserts of Argentina, Mongolia and, above all, China. Despite this, scholars have probably uncovered only a small proportion (between 10 and 25 per cent) of all dinosaur species to exist. They did not all live at the same time, as different species were continuously dying out and emerging.

By 312 million years ago, the first reptiles, which had evolved from amphibians, began to emerge. Unlike amphibians, they laid hard-shelled eggs on land and had tougher scaly skin, as well as stronger legs and larger brains. Around 240 million years ago, the first dinosaurs appeared. The earliest known species is probably *Nyasasaurus parringtoni*, which was first discovered in Tanzania, and stood over 2 metres (6.5 feet) tall. By this stage, Earth was in the first period of the Mesozoic Era – the Triassic. All of the continents were in a single land mass called Pangaea. The desert conditions and hot and dry climate of the time were ideal for reptiles, helping dinosaurs to become the dominant animal group and spread across Pangaea. Dinosaurs were so successful because they were adept at gathering food, be it by eating plant life or through hunting and scavenging other animals.

Around 201 million years ago, a series of massive earthquakes heralded the end of the Triassic Period and the beginning of the Jurassic. Pangaea was torn asunder, creating the supercontinents of Laurasia and Gondwana. At this time, many dinosaur species became extinct, but the more diverse geographical conditions ultimately led to an increase in their numbers overall. Falling temperatures and greater rainfall led to more abundant plant life, which created a food source for the sauropods, a family of huge plant-eating dinosaurs. They had long necks to browse for food from trees and strong teeth to grind down tough, fibrous plants. This family included a subgroup called the Titanosaurs, which were the largest of the dinosaurs. The biggest of them may have been the *Argentinosaurus*, classified in 1993. No complete skeleton has been found, but analysis of recovered bones found it was over 36 metres (about 120 feet) long and weighed up to 100,000 kilograms (100 tons). The Jurassic also saw the evolution of the Thyreophora, a group of herbivorous dinosaurs distinguished by armoured plates along their bodies; the most famous of these was the 9-metre-long (about 30 feet) *Stegosaurus*, which also had a spiked tail to ward off predators.

The final period of the Mesozoic was the Cretaceous, which began 145 million years ago. It saw the supercontinents split further apart, leading to the beginning of the formation of Earth's present-day continents. This meant that dinosaurs became more diverse to adapt to changing conditions. These included two of the most iconic dinosaurs. The first was the *Triceratops*, which weighed up to 12,000 kilograms (12 tons), ate plants with its beak-like mouth and had three horns and a large, bony, frilled head. This defended it from the carnivorous *Tyrannosaurus*, which could grow to 12 metres (nearly 40 feet) long, reaching weights of 14,000 kilograms (14 tons). Moving around on its rear legs, the *Tyrannosaurus* had powerful jaws bristling with sixty 20-centimetre-long (around 8 inches) teeth and was one of the most fearsome predators to walk the Earth.

Palaeontological Ponderings

There are endless debates about the purpose of dinosaurs' anatomical features; for example, the *Stegosaurus*'s bony fins along its back. Initially it was believed they were for self-defence, but by the later twentieth century palaeontologists theorized they helped to regulate body temperature; more recently, it has been argued they developed to attract mates.

Around 66 million years ago, there was a mass extinction of the majority of dinosaur species. Many other species also became extinct, including the flying pterosaurs and large marine reptiles such as the ichthyosaurs and the plesiosaurs. There are numerous explanations for this event, including disease, heatwaves, extreme cold temperatures, volcanic activity, mammals eating dinosaur eggs or even X-rays striking the Earth from a star going supernova. The most commonly accepted explanation was that an asteroid more than 10 kilometres (over 6 miles) in diameter struck the Earth, which led to rapid climate change, huge tsunamis, volcanic eruptions and earthquakes. This theory was proved by the discovery of deposits of iridium, which is common in asteroids, dating to this time. It may have struck the Earth near Chicxulub in Mexico, the centre of a crater that was over 160 kilometres (around 100 miles) wide. Many fish, particularly those that lived in the deep sea, survived, as did other reptiles like the crocodilians, snakes and lizards, as well as amphibians and mammals. After the Mesozoic Period ended, only one group of dinosaurs remained: the avians, which would evolve into birds.

SHARKS

Over 500 species of shark exist today, ranging in size from the 20-centimetre-long dwarf lantern shark to the massive whale shark, which is the largest extant fish and can reach a length of 18 metres (about 60 feet) and a weight of 14,000 kilograms (14 tons). They differ from bony fish in many ways. Most significant is that their skeletons are made of cartilage, which is half as dense as bone, allowing them to swim longer distances while expending less energy. Few families of animals can rival the shark's longevity. Based on recovery of fossilized scales, the very earliest sharks appeared around 420 million years ago, long before the emergence of the dinosaurs. Since then, there have been at least 3,000 species of shark. However, assembling an accurate record of shark evolution and precisely determining their appearance is often difficult because for the most part only their teeth and scales fossilize, while their soft cartilaginous skeletons disintegrate.

Around 359 million years ago, the Devonian Period ended and the Carboniferous began; for the previous 20 million years ocean oxygen levels had been dropping, perhaps due to volcanic activity, leading 75 per cent of all species to become extinct. Sharks survived. The Carboniferous Period saw them branch out into forty-five different families (there are now just nine) and evolve a range of different features. They include the *Falcatus*, males of which had a sword-like appendage that curved over their head; the *Helicoprion*, whose lower teeth were arranged into a spiral that resembled a circular saw; and the *Stethacanthus*, which had an anvil-shaped dorsal fin whose precise purpose is still undetermined. Another mass extinction event occurred 252 million years ago at the beginning of the Triassic Period, when rising temperatures led to 96 per cent of all marine life dying out. Sharks survived both this event, and another that occurred around 201 million years ago, when the Triassic Period ended and the Jurassic began. When the majority of dinosaurs were wiped out as the Cretaceous Period ended 66 million years ago, sharks persisted. However, many shark species did become extinct. Those that survived tended to be smaller and live in deeper waters. Eventually, larger species would emerge, and sharks began to reappear in shallower waters.

The most fearsome was megalodon, which dates back to around 23 million years ago. It was an apex predator that reached over 25 metres (82 feet) in length. Large enough to prey on whales, its bite diameter was around 3 metres (10 feet) and its large, thick teeth reached lengths of 17 centimetres (nearly 7 inches). Impressive though it was, megalodon became extinct 3.6 million years ago. Changing climates disrupted its food supply and it faced increased competition for prey from other, smaller sharks, as well as carnivorous whales.

One of the reasons that sharks have been able to survive where other families of animals have not is their ability to hunt a range of prey across different habitats. Most sharks have extremely acute senses. Their nostrils can detect smells independently, which means they can determine the direction a scent came from. They can hear splashing from a long distance and have sensory receptors (called ampullae of Lorenzini) on their heads that detect electromagnetic fields created by other animals. Hammerheads, the most recent modern family of sharks to appear, between 45 and 23 million years ago, have particularly strong senses. Their flattened, hammer-shaped heads have more widely spaced eyes that give better vision and space for more sensory receptors. They may also use their heads to ram prey and pin it to the seabed.

Furthermore, many sharks are extremely rapid swimmers, enabling them to circle and quickly strike at their prey (often attacking from below), and bite at it with their sharp, triangular teeth. The fastest is the shortfin mako, capable of a top speed of 74 kilometres per hour (46 miles per hour). Not all sharks are so fast. The Somniosidae, known as the sleeper sharks, move extremely slowly. They include the Greenland shark, which lives in the depths of the North Atlantic and Arctic Ocean and swims at less than 3 kilometres per hour (2 miles per hour). It is the longest-living vertebrate species; radiocarbon dating revealed they can live three to five centuries.

Many sharks will also feed on a wide variety of other animals. The great white shark, for example, eats seals, sea turtles, sea lions, dolphins and small whales, as well as scavenging. Belying the image created by films like *Jaws* (1975), sharks have no great predilection for eating humans. On the contrary, sharks prefer animals with more blubber – most attacks on humans are the result of mistaken identity. Three species of shark (the whale, basking and megamouth) are filter-feeders. They feed by swimming through the ocean with their mouths open, filtering out small fish and creatures like shrimp, algae and plankton from the water.

THE CROCODILIANS

The earliest ancestors of the crocodilians appeared over 200 million years ago. Along with the birds, they are the only surviving Archosaurs ('ruling reptiles'), a group of animals that includes dinosaurs and pterosaurs. The first crocodilians evolved into today's crocodiles, alligators, caimans and gharials (the latter eat mainly fish and at up to 6 metres [20 feet] are the longest of the family). These semi-aquatic animals live mainly in the tropics and kill around 1,000 people every year, forty times more than sharks do.

Although sharks have survived mass extinctions, they now face one of the biggest threats: humans. Every year over 100 million sharks die at the hands of mankind. This is particularly damaging because sharks have slow growth and reproduction rates compared to other fish, making it hard for them to replenish their numbers. Sharks have often been hunted for food, and in parts of Asia their fins are particularly treasured. In addition, their liver oil was once a valuable commodity primarily used as an industrial lubricant as well as an ingredient in cosmetics. Millions of sharks are also killed accidentally when they become tangled up in fishing nets. As a result, around a quarter of shark species are threatened with extinction.

ARCHAEOPTERYX

In 1861, two fossils were discovered that revolutionized natural history, setting in motion decades of scholarly debate. That year, the German palaeontologist Hermann von Meyer (1801–69) reported a fossilized feather that had recently been discovered in a limestone quarry near the Bavarian town of Solnhofen. He later proposed that it belonged to a creature that he named *Archaeopteryx*, from the ancient Greek for 'old wing'. A few months later, a nearly complete *Archaeopteryx* skeleton was unearthed near the town of Langenaltheim, around 6 kilometres (4 miles) away from the original find. Many believed this *Archaeopteryx* was the *Urvogel* (German for 'original bird'), the common ancestor of the nearly 10,000 extant species of birds, who are the only living dinosaurs.

Following the discoveries of 1861, eleven more fossils found in that vicinity have been classified as being remains of an *Archaeopteryx*. One of them had been actually found in 1855 but was initially believed to belong to a pterodactyl before being classified as an *Archaeopteryx*. They all date to around 150 million years ago, during the late Jurassic Period, when Europe was an archipelago of islands in a shallow, tropical sea located closer to the equator than it is today. Study of the *Archaeopteryx* fossils showed that it was about 50 centimetres (20 inches) long (roughly the size of a magpie) and shared features common to both birds and dinosaurs. This was a 'transitional fossil', something that captures the evolutionary process of one animal group diverging sharply from its ancestors. It provided a neat proof for the recently posited theory of evolution.

The *Archaeopteryx* shared features with carnivorous dinosaurs. Unlike birds, it sported a long tail and had sharp conical teeth that it used to eat small reptiles, mammals and insects. Like many birds, it had three forward-facing claws, but its most obviously avian feature was its feathers (which later analysis showed were jet-black). One of the main purposes of feathers is to help with flight, as they provide a solid yet lightweight surface that pushes against the air. This was not their original purpose, as many flightless dinosaurs had them. They first evolved them to help insulate their bodies or repel water. The flying ability of the *Archaeopteryx* has frequently been brought into question; some scholars doubted it was capable of true flight, and suggested it was only able to glide down from trees. Like extant flightless birds such as the kiwi, the *Archaeopteryx* had a flat, short sternum. It did not have 'keels', bony extensions to the sternum that most birds have, which anchor the powerful muscles that flap their wings and achieve flight. In 2018, a powerful X-ray of three *Archaeopteryx* specimens showed that their bone density was thin enough for them to have achieved flight. But its bones were most similar to a quail's or pheasant's, suggesting it could only fly in short bursts, possibly either to escape from a predator or capture prey. This analysis also showed that the *Archaeopteryx* skeletons were rich with blood vessels, meaning their metabolism was similar to birds.

The early Cretaceous Period gave rise to species that more closely resembled modern birds. Their anatomy changed to make them more suited to flight, including a shortening of their tails and more aerodynamic plumage. DNA analysis shows that recognizably modern avians had evolved by the mid- to late Cretaceous, for example the ancestors of flamingos. After the mass extinction event that led to the extinction of most dinosaurs, only the avians would survive and then diversify further. Some would specialize in maritime environments, eating fish by diving or wading, while others lived in trees. The disappearance of the dinosaurs left a gap that was filled with large, flightless predatory birds that reached heights of over 2 metres (6.5 feet).

During the early twenty-first century, a series of discoveries have been made in rock formations of Northeast China that challenge the status of the *Archaeopteryx* as the first bird. In 2011, a species called *Xiaotingia zhengi* was classified. It was a feathered reptile around 0.6 metres (2 feet) long with clawed forelimbs and sharp teeth, and was 5 million years older than the *Archaeopteryx*. Its finders argued that it was part of a group of dinosaurs called the Deinonychosauria. They also claimed the *Archaeopteryx* was part of this group, meaning it could no longer be classified as avian. The next year, further study confirmed that the *Archaeopteryx* was indeed more closely related to birds than other dinosaurs, and the reclassification was rejected. It is now clear that during the late Jurassic there were several species of dinosaur developing feathers and other avian features. This shows just how difficult it is to pinpoint evolutionary transitions using the fossil record. For now, the *Archaeopteryx* is still recognized as the species that could be definitively classified as the first member of the bird family, although further discoveries may unseat it from its position as the *Urvogel*, or first known bird.

THE PTEROSAURS

The pterosaurs are a family of extinct reptiles that were the first vertebrates to fly. They emerged during the late Triassic, over 250 million years ago, and had wings made of a membrane of skin and muscle. The largest of them, *Quetzalcoatlus northropi*, had a wingspan of over 10 metres (33 feet).

Darwin's Finches

On 2 October 1836, HMS *Beagle* docked in Cornwall after a round-the-world voyage of nearly five years. Launched as a warship in 1820, it had been reassigned as a survey vessel in 1825 and from 1826 to 1830 it had charted Patagonia and Tierra del Fuego in South America. The *Beagle* set out on its second voyage in 1831 under the command of Robert FitzRoy (1805–65), an aristocratic Royal Navy officer who would go on to be a pioneering meteorologist and serve as governor of New Zealand. His mission was to continue to survey the coastline of South America. Before the voyage, FitzRoy and his family had grown concerned he may become isolated and depressed without learned companionship on such a long voyage, so they sought a 'gentleman naturalist' to accompany him on board. The man who sailed with him when the *Beagle* set out on 27 December 1831 was a recent graduate of the University of Cambridge called Charles Darwin. During the voyage, Darwin would make a series of observations of animals that led to the shaping of a theory that revolutionized the way people viewed the natural world. Instrumental to this were the birds he saw while on the Galápagos Islands.

Darwin was the second son of a society doctor. He had abandoned his own studies in medicine at the University of Edinburgh after becoming more interested in natural history. In 1828, he moved to Cambridge in preparation for being a Church of England parson, a position that would allow him to combine an ecclesiastical career with continuing his scientific research. While at Cambridge, Darwin continued his studies of the natural world, collecting beetles and undertaking some geological surveying. Six months after gaining his degree, Darwin left England on the *Beagle*. His position on the ship was funded by his uncle, a scion of the wealthy Wedgwood family, who had made a fortune in pottery. This meant that the specimens Darwin collected would be his alone, and he would be able to pursue whatever interests he saw fit. Despite suffering from seasickness, Darwin was incredibly productive while on board the *Beagle*, writing a 770-page diary, making 1,750 pages of notes and collecting 5,436 skins, bones and carcasses.

The *Beagle* arrived in South America in February 1832, docking at Salvador in north-eastern Brazil. Thanks to his supernumerary position, Darwin was able to make independent expeditions into the interior. It was in Argentina, which the *Beagle* began charting in August, that Darwin's research began to gather pace. He rode inland into Patagonia, where he viewed armadillos and 'ostriches' (it was actually a related species called the rhea). He also located fossils of the bones of extinct prehistoric mammals, including *Megatherium* (a giant sloth). These specimens led Darwin to begin to consider why these species had met extinction. After reaching Tierra del Fuego in December, the *Beagle* continued its work, before beginning its survey of the west coast of South America in June 1834. Then, on 16 September that year, the *Beagle* reached the Galápagos Islands, an archipelago nearly 1,000 kilometres (about 600 miles) west of Ecuador. Although Darwin only remained there for five weeks, his stay would have an indelible imprint on his work.

Darwin travelled to four of the Galápagos Islands.

On each, he captured brown birds between 10 and 20 centimetres (4 to 8 inches) long. At first, he did not believe they were related because they varied so much. That they were distinct, yet related, species was only pointed out to him after he returned home. Nonetheless, these were his eponymous 'finches' (despite their name, they are not classified as part of the finch family, but another one called the tanagers). Darwin eventually theorized that they all had their origin in a common ancestor that ate seeds from the ground (where it came from is still debated – the Caribbean and the South American mainland have been proposed). Over time, diet had determined variation in the size and form of their bills – some were suited for insects (with the woodpecker finch using cactus spines or twigs to dislodge its prey from trees), some for seeds, some for cacti and one for fruits and buds. This observation would eventually help prove to him that it was not God that determined the formation of new species, but adaptation to environment.

After leaving the Galápagos, the *Beagle* travelled home via Tahiti, New Zealand, Australia and South Africa. After Darwin arrived back in England in 1836, he published a description of his voyage to great acclaim in 1839. Having married in the same year, he retreated to the village of Downe, near London, in 1842. There he worked on his theories of evolution and in 1859 published *On the Origin of Species*. This discussed (with reference to the birds of the Galápagos) how natural selection had led to the creation of the world's animal life. In doing so, he challenged the concept that God or some other divine force had created all life forms. This sparked fractious debate, but by the end of the nineteenth century evolution was widely accepted across the scientific community. Darwin remained at Downe and, before his death in 1883, published works on evolution, plants and the impact of earthworms on soil.

The Galápagos Islands became emblematic of Darwin's theories, and scientists and researchers would continue to travel there to study its flora and fauna. DNA analysis of the finches proved Darwin right – they all descended from a common ancestor that had arrived in the Galápagos 2 to 3 million years ago. Their differences are partly due to variation in a gene called ALX1, which forms facial and head bones. A fourteenth species of Darwin's finch was found on Cocos Island, around 800 kilometres (500 miles) away from its relatives on the Galápagos Islands. Despite loss of habitat and the introduction of invasive species, none of Darwin's finches are yet extinct (though the mangrove finch and the medium tree finch are critically endangered). Indeed, interbreeding may even be leading to the creation of a new species of Darwin's finch, showing how the process of natural selection and evolution is a dynamic and continuous one.

THE GREAT APES

. . . .

Humans are classified as part of the great ape family, also known as the hominids, which includes seven other species: the bonobo, the chimpanzee, the eastern and western gorilla, and the Bornean, Sumatran and Tapanuli orangutan. These great apes are all part of the primates, an order of mammals that arose around 60 million years ago. The first primates evolved to live and move through trees of tropical forests (as well as gather food there), although many species later adapted to live in more varied conditions such as savanna and desert. All primates share stronger vision and greater dexterity than other animals, and similarities between them and humans have been noticed since ancient times. When the Swedish botanist Carl Linnaeus (1707–78) was categorizing the natural world during the eighteenth century, he classified humans as primates in his taxonomy of animal species.

Once Charles Darwin's (1809–82) theory of evolution

became widely accepted during the second half of the nineteenth century, it became clear that humans must have some relations in the animal world, and possibly some kind of common ancestor. His colleague Thomas Henry Huxley (1825–95) argued that humans were close to two species of great ape – the gorilla and the chimpanzee. He then proved the anatomical similarities between their brains and those of humans. Since then, evolutionary biologists have been searching for the last common ancestor that humans and the great apes share. It is still unknown what this common ancestor of the great apes looked like, although it is likely that it lived in Africa and was a small, long-armed primate possibly weighing around 5 kilograms (11 pounds).

Apes, also known as the hominoids, first emerged over 36 million years ago, during the Miocene epoch, probably somewhere in Africa, although they also settled across Eurasia. Eventually, over one hundred species of ape arose, and they shared features such as mobile limb joints, a strong grip and not having a tail. Around 17 million years ago, the gibbons, a family of eighteen species also known as lesser apes, split off to form their own family, characterized by being smaller and having longer arms.

Over 13 million years ago, the orangutans (which means 'person of the forest' in Malay) split off from the rest of the great apes. Although now native to just the islands of Borneo and Sumatra, they once lived across East Asia, ranging as far afield as southern China. They are distinguished by reddish-brown hair and the cheek pads of males, which they use to attract mates and deter rivals. Unlike the rest of the great apes, which tend to live in communities, the three species of orangutans are mostly solitary. They spend the majority of their time in trees, and move by swinging from branch to branch using their arms (a technique called brachiation). The gorillas set off on their own evolutionary path 8.5 to 12 million years ago, splitting into two species. The eastern gorilla, which lives in modern-day Uganda, Rwanda and eastern Democratic Republic of the Congo, became the largest of the great apes, with males often weighing around 225 kilograms (496 pounds) with a standing height of 1.7 metres (5.6 feet). Slightly smaller is the western gorilla, which lives in West Africa.

Early humans split off from the rest of the great apes 5.5 to 7 million years ago. From the ape-like family of species called *Australopithecus*, they developed into the genus *Homo*, the family which includes modern humans. A major point of difference was their gradual switch to permanent bipedalism (walking on two legs). This shortened their forelimbs but meant they could make more complex tools. Another evolutionary advancement was their speaking ability, which was far more developed than other species. This helped them spread out from Africa to eventually settle every corner of the world. Over the millennia numerous species of early humans evolved and became extinct until the arrival of *Homo sapiens*, the first anatomically modern fossils of which were found in Morocco, dating back to 330,000 years ago.

The remaining great apes, the chimpanzee and the bonobo, were on the same evolutionary trajectory until they split into two species 1 to 1.5 million years ago. Chimpanzees, which live in the forests and savannas of tropical Africa, are skilled at brachiation. Their diet is more varied than other non-human great apes – in addition to vegetation and insects, they are also known to eat eggs, carrion, other mammals and even engage in cannibalism. They live in communities of between twenty and a hundred, and are often engaged in hostilities, with violent attacks and raids common. The bonobo was initially known as the pygmy chimpanzee and was not recognized as its own species until 1933. They live along the south bank of the Congo River and are generally more peaceable and sociable than chimpanzees, with less conflict between groups, possibly because food is more abundant where they live.

Genetic sequencing has shown that humans are closer to chimpanzees and bonobos than other great apes. Their entire genome sequence differs by only 1.2 per cent (compared to a 1.6 per cent difference with gorillas and 3.1 per cent with orangutans). Furthermore, study of their behaviour has shown the links between great apes and humans. All of the great apes can recognize themselves in the mirror – something no other animal can do. They can make and use simple tools to help them gather food and water. They also have advanced communication skills compared to other animals. In the wild, great apes, particularly chimpanzees, use a range of vocalizations or drumming on trees to communicate over long distances. In captivity, humans have taught them semi-linguistic communication using sign language, tokens and symbols, while some great apes have even mimicked human speech. While some researchers believe this is a form of language, others argue that they are just making gestures or performing in return for a reward.

Today the non-human great apes face a range of problems including habitat loss, disease, logging, loss of land for plantations, forest fires and being hunted for bushmeat. This means they are all endangered species, placing humanity's closest relations at the risk of extinction.

'LUCY'

Australopithecus afarensis is an extinct early human that emerged around 3.6 million years ago in East Africa; it was bipedal but had long arms suited for tree-climbing. Its most famous specimen is 'Lucy' (named after a Beatles song), discovered in Ethiopia in 1974, a set of fossilized bones 3.2 million years old.

2

HOME AND WAR

DOGS

. . . .

Two million years ago, early humans banded together to form hunter-gatherer societies. Ranging across territories of up to 1,300 square kilometres (500 square miles) in groups of about a dozen to around a hundred, they were almost constantly on the move in search of food. Using simple tools and weapons, they hunted and scavenged animals, as well as gathering plants. All humans lived this way until about 12,000 years ago, when they began to establish settled agricultural communities, which first occurred in the region of Mesopotamia (in modern-day Iraq). This was made possible by the domestication of wild plants and animals, a process that was one of the foundations of human control and exploitation of the natural world. Centuries before this happened, humans had already domesticated their first species of animal: the dog.

Dogs have been living with humans for at least 15,000 years and perhaps as long as 40,000. Many questions remain about exactly where, when and how they were domesticated. What is certain is that dogs are domesticated variants of the wild grey wolf. There are two main theories as to how dogs were domesticated. The first is that a wolf-like species began approaching hunter-gatherer bands hoping to be given food, and over time the friendliest ones became attached to these communities and became their companions. The second is that humans actively began to tame and selectively breed these wild wolves so they could use them as hunters, trackers and guards. Their natural ability made them ideally suited for these tasks – dogs have a highly acute sense of smell and their hearing is nearly twice as sensitive as a human's. They also have a strong bite and are able to tear flesh. Over the generations, the natural pack mentality of dogs was transferred to humans and they developed a highly attuned ability to read emotional cues from humans.

When and where dogs were first domesticated is unknown. Some scientists suggest Central Asia around 13,000 BC, while others propose somewhere in China around 15,300 BC. There is evidence for even older domestication in the form of footprints of a child walking alongside a dog, dating back to 26,000 years ago, found in the Chauvet Cave in southern France, while in the Goyet Caves of Belgium the skull of a primitive version of a dog over 36,500 years old has been found. In 2016, it was suggested that the domestication of dogs did not occur in one place, but separately, from distinct populations of wolves, on opposite sides of Eurasia. The dogs that were domesticated in East Asia then migrated west with their human masters and largely supplanted the earliest

European dogs. Regardless of the precise timing, by the time humans began to create the first permanent farming communities, dogs were already well established as their companions. After other wild animals were domesticated as livestock, dogs were utilized to herd and guard them.

Dogs became ever more integrated into human society and culture. Excavation of Stone Age and Bronze Age tombs in the Americas, Asia, Europe and Africa showed that they began to be buried with humans, possibly so they could continue to serve them after death. The ancient Egyptians were particularly loyal to their dogs – often mummifying them when they died and shaving off their eyebrows as a sign of mourning. In ancient civilizations from Mesopotamia to China, figurines of dogs were made and buried near buildings to ward off bad luck. Dogs often figured prominently in ancient mythology, with strong associations with loyalty and devotion. For example, in the ancient Sanskrit epic the *Mahabharata*, one of its protagonists, King Yudhishthira, is accompanied by his loyal dog as he makes the ascent into Heaven. When asked to abandon him to gain entry, he refuses – it was this action that shows Yudhishthira's worthiness. In the *Odyssey*, when the protagonist, Odysseus, returns home to Ithaca after his epic journey, no one recognizes him save for Argos, his faithful dog.

BALTO

In 1925, diphtheria struck the Alaskan town of Nome. After local authorities had desperately appealed for antitoxins to prevent thousands of deaths, they were shipped to the port of Seward and then taken by train to Nenana. From there, a relay of dog sleds carried the received medical supplies 1,085 kilometres (674 miles), in freezing conditions, to Nome. On 2 February, a team led by a Siberian husky called Balto arrived, saving the day. After Balto died in 1933, his body was stuffed and put on display at the Cleveland Museum of Natural History.

Millennia of selective breeding by humans have led to the creation of the most diverse animal species on the planet, from the tiny chihuahua to the mighty Great Dane. Some breeds have become highly specialized for certain environments. For example, breeds that work as sled dogs in the Arctic, which have origins dating back to 9,500 years ago, are able to eat blubber, can work in low-oxygen conditions and have a strong ability to regulate their body temperature. Most modern dog breeds exhibit physical features that show their original purpose, such as the short-legged dachshunds that were able to pursue badgers into their underground burrows, the stocky, powerful and large-headed bull dogs that were used in the lamentable practice of bull-baiting, or the bloodhound, whose acute sense of smell was used to track animals (it is now also used to sniff out explosives and drugs). Toy dogs were bred for their small size and served as companions and status symbols for elites (as well as keeping their laps warm). Although this process has accentuated many useful features, it has also had the unintended effect of creating health problems in many dog breeds, such as the breathing problems that bedevil pugs. By the second half of the nineteenth century, breeds had begun to be more rigorously classified, with standards of ideal physical appearance created for each one, and pedigrees of individual dogs diligently recorded and registered. As of 2018, the Kennel Club of the United Kingdom (the oldest body of its kind) officially recognizes 221 distinct breeds. Regardless of their appearance, dogs are a reminder that to thrive and prosper humanity has always needed the help of other animals.

PIGS

Pork is the most consumed meat in the world (closely followed by poultry), and there is a global population of over 1 billion pigs. The domestication of the pig from the Eurasian wild boar took place independently, in Anatolia and East Asia, over 9,000 years ago. Five hundred years later they were introduced to Europe, then Africa. Around 3000 BC, pigs came to Oceania, accompanying the people who settled the islands of the South Pacific. Pigs had many virtues as a livestock animal; they provided meat and fat, while their skin could be made into leather and their hair into brushes. Pigs could also live in a wide range of habitats and, as they were omnivores, ate a wide range of food, including household waste and scraps.

In many regions of the world, there are religious taboos against eating pork, which are particularly strong in the Middle East. During the mid-fifth century BC, the Torah, the holy book of Judaism, was composed. It contained the dietary requirements for the Jewish people, and specified that they should only eat animals that have cloven hooves and chew the cud (for example, cows and sheep). This precluded them from eating pork, which was deemed to be 'unclean'. The roots of why this rule was put into place are much debated; some scholars believe the law was included to create a separate identity for the Jewish people, while others link it to the perception of the pig as being unhygienic because it will eat anything and wallows in mud (they do this because they lack sweat glands, so it keeps them cool as well as deterring mosquitoes and protecting their skin from the sun). The Quran, revealed to the Prophet Muhammad (c. AD 570–632) in the early seventh century AD, also declared pork impure and forbidden (although it could be eaten in an emergency). Likewise, most Hindus and Buddhists avoid pork as part of their generally vegetarian diet. Christians did not adopt the food restrictions of the Old Testament (with the exception of the Churches that arose in modern-day Ethiopia) and so were free to eat pork.

THE PIG WAR OF 1859

The San Juan Islands are in the Pacific Northwest of the USA, close to the Canadian border. In 1859, they were the site of a stand-off between the USA and the British Empire. At that time, the status of the islands was unclear. To stake a claim, a British firm sent an employee called Charles Griffin to run a ranch on San Juan Island. Americans also settled it. One of them, Lyman Cutlar, planted a potato patch. On 15 June 1859, Cutlar saw one of Griffin's pigs eating his crops and shot it. When British authorities threatened to arrest Cutlar, the American settlers requested protection from their government. On 27 July, US Army soldiers landed on San Juan Island and declared it American territory. The British then sent warships to the area. To de-escalate the volatile situation, the US president sent a representative for talks with the local British governor. They agreed a truce and joint military occupations of the islands until a settlement was reached. This continued until 1872, when an international panel awarded the islands to the USA.

By the late eighteenth century, pig-farming had spread to every continent in the world – being brought to the Americas in 1493 during Christopher Columbus's (1451–1506) second voyage, and to Australia in 1788 by the First Fleet, which established the penal colony that became the first European settlement there. Coincidentally, salted pork meat would have been one of the main food sources on these, and other, European voyages. During the nineteenth century, the farming of pigs became increasingly intensive. Breeders sought to produce pigs that would gain weight quickly and efficiently. One of them was the 'Large White', which was developed in Yorkshire and has since become the most popular pig breed in the world. As demand for pork has increased, farmers have responded by trying to maximize output by moving their pigs indoors to make it easier to regulate temperate and collect waste, packing the animals tightly together. This means that their meat has become more affordable for many, but at the cost of the pigs living in an environment that denies their natural instincts to be sociable, wallow and root for food.

HORSES

. . . .

The wheel is one of the most significant inventions in history. Its first use was not for transport, but in the manufacture of pottery; the Mesopotamians were using it to shape clay by the fifth millennium BC. From around 3500 BC, it began to be used to make simple wheeled vehicles, which developed into more complex carts and wagons. At first, these were pulled by oxen. Although strong and sturdy, they lacked the dynamism of the animal that revolutionized transport: the horse. It combined speed and endurance, enabling humans to travel longer distances while carrying heavier loads. It was also used to power machinery and until the twentieth century was fundamental to warfare.

All horses descend from a lamb-sized hoofed mammal called *Eohippus* that arose about 50 million years ago and ate leaves and lived in the forest. Most of the process that saw it evolve into a horse by 4.5 million years ago took place in North America. It grew in size, its legs lengthened, and the central toe evolved into a hoof. Its teeth and digestive system adapted to grazing for grass, which meant it flourished on the plains that formed in North America when the climate became drier. Around

2 million years ago, the horse crossed from the Americas via the Bering land bridge, spreading out across Eurasia and Africa. The horse disappeared from its ancestral homeland 10,000 to 8,000 years ago as a result of disease or being hunted into extinction. It would not reappear in the Americas until its reintroduction by Spanish colonists in the late fifteenth century.

Horses probably began to be domesticated on the Eurasian Steppe, in modern-day Kazakhstan and Ukraine, as early as 5000 BC. At first, they were raised for meat and milk. It was not until around 3000 BC, when evidence from fossilized horse skulls shows worn-down teeth, indicating use of a bit, that horses were being regularly ridden. Over the next five millennia, humans selectively bred horses to serve a range of different functions, leading to the creation of over 300 breeds.

One of the primary uses of horses was in agriculture; they were used to pull ploughs and other farming equipment. By the fourth century BC, they were also being used to power machinery by being harnessed to mills that performed tasks such as grinding grain or pumping water. Even more significant was their use in transport, allowing people to travel long distances and bring goods to market. From ancient times, they were also used to haul boats along waterways. Finally, pre-modern communication relied heavily on horse-borne couriers. In the nineteenth century, the mechanization of agriculture, industry and transport, as well as the introduction of the electrical telegraph, led to a great reduction in the social and economic importance of horses.

It was in the military sphere that horses had their greatest impact. Their pace and balance, accentuated by selective breeding, combined with their strong sense of direction, visual memory and ability to respond to physical and verbal cues from their rider. The Steppe peoples, the nomadic herders who lived on the vast plains that covered much of Mongolia and Central Asia, were the first to domesticate horses, and they became highly skilled at using them in warfare. By around 2000 BC, they had developed the composite bow, which was made from wood, horn and sinew. It was small enough to be fired from horseback, but its design made it extremely powerful, and it was lethal at ranges of over 450 metres (500 yards). When combined with the Steppe horse, a nimble, sturdy and indefatigable breed, peoples like the Scythians, Huns and Magyars became feared across Asia and Europe.

The first chariots were developed around 2000 BC, and they were eventually used across Eurasia and Africa. Pulled by horses, often in teams of up to four, they served as mobile platforms for archers that could travel at speeds of 30 kilometres per hour (nearly 20 miles per hour). In 1275 BC, the largest chariot battle in history, between the Egyptians and the Hittites, took place at Kadesh, in modern-day Syria. Five thousand chariots rode into battle, but no one achieved a decisive victory, leading the two powers to make a peace treaty (the world's first recorded one). From this point, chariots declined as they required even terrain, and the breeding of stronger, larger horses that could carry heavily armed warriors into battle made them obsolete (although they carried on being used in China until the third century BC). Replacing the chariot were massed cavalry charges, often used as shock attacks to break enemy infantry.

The next innovation to transform the use of horses was the stirrup. The first versions may have appeared in Asia as early as the fourth century BC, but they were being widely used in China by the fifth century AD. They spread across Asia, and were in use across much of Europe by the eighth century. They were vital because they gave riders far greater control of the horse, and provided them with the stability to use weapons such as the sword or lance. Furthermore, when combined with more sophisticated harnessing, they allowed horses to carry heavier loads.

During the thirteenth century, the Mongols created the largest continuous empire the world has ever seen, extending from Korea to western Russia. Its foundation was the horse, along with the stirrup and the composite bow. Mongol warriors, who each had three to four mounts, could cover around 160 kilometres (100 miles) per day. Thanks to their training and strict code of conduct, they could launch rapid coordinated attacks against the enemy. By the time the Mongol Empire had begun to decline and start breaking apart, in the mid-fourteenth century, gunpowder weapons were beginning to be used, which radically changed the role of the horse.

BUCEPHALUS

Alexander the Great (356–323 BC) established an empire that extended from Egypt to India. His companion since childhood was his horse Bucephalus (meaning 'ox-head' after the shape of its brand), a huge black stallion. In 326 BC, Bucephalus died at the Battle of the Hydaspes, in modern-day Pakistan; Alexander honoured him by naming the city he founded nearby Bucephalia.

The invention of cannons and firearms made the heavily armoured knights of the medieval era obsolete. Although the mounted charge was still being used as late as the nineteenth century, cavalry generally transitioned to being used for skirmishing, raiding, reconnaissance and patrol. Horses remained vital to warfare – particularly through being used to haul light artillery pieces around the battlefield. They also continued to play an important military role as beasts of burden – before the advent of the steam railway and the internal combustion engine, no large army could operate without horses to carry their equipment. Indeed, even amid the mechanized slaughter of World War II, over 7 million horses were used, particularly on the Eastern Front.

CHICKENS

. . . .

In 490 BC, a Persian army of 20,000 invaded Greece, landing near Marathon, a town 29 kilometres (18 miles) from Athens. The Persian Empire was the greatest power in the world at the time, extending from the Indus Valley to Arabia to North Africa to the Balkans. The Persians had grown angry with Greek city states after they had supported rebellions against their rule in Anatolia. To prevent future meddling, their ruler, Emperor Darius the Great (*c.* 550–486 BC), invaded Greece. An Athenian politician and general, Themistocles (524–459 BC), led the opposition. As he was marching his force of 10,000 to Marathon, he was said to have came across two roosters fighting. Inspired, he urged his men to emulate their combative spirit and fight not for their land or their gods, but for the glory of victory. The Greeks, despite having no archers or cavalry, forced the Persians to flee to their ships through the sheer will of their massed infantry. The Persian threat re-emerged a decade later but once again the Greeks won victory. Chickens often symbolize courage and aggression, yet they have also become associated with timidity and cowardice. This echoes the changing perception of chickens; from being fighting birds and an important part of ritual, to being bywords for the worst aspects of intensive agriculture.

Chickens were domesticated around 7,400 years ago in South East Asia and India. They descend primarily from the red junglefowl. It is mostly shy, not a particularly able flyer and rarely strays far from its home territory. Over time, chickens became more sociable with people and by the second millennium BC had spread out into China, Oceania, the Middle East and Africa. The Phoenicians introduced them to Europe during the eighth century BC.

In the wild, chickens form flocks under the leadership of a dominant male. There is a constant struggle to be at the top of the hierarchy, and violent struggles between roosters are common. To the present day, humans across the world have made use of this aggression by pitting roosters against each other in combat. The procedure is broadly similar worldwide: two roosters, sometimes with blades attached to their claws, are made to fight in circular pits until one dies or is incapacitated. Gambling on the outcome is common, and birds are often given drugs to make them stronger or more aggressive.

While roosters became symbols of virility and masculinity, female chickens are more associated with fertility. Until the last century, hens were primarily kept for their egg-laying capability. This is because hens will lay eggs even if they have not mated with a rooster (although they may become 'broody' and sit on unfertilized eggs and stop laying). The ancient Egyptians were the first to take steps towards artificially increasing fertility. By the mid-eighth century BC, they were building artificial incubation complexes with tunnels and vents that kept the temperature and humidity at levels that meant eggs would hatch without the involvement of their mothers, who would thus be free to lay more. The ancient Romans were also enthusiastic chicken-keepers, not only eating them but using them in rituals. An official called the *pullarius* was in charge of keeping sacred chickens. Before events such as battles, grain was cast before the chickens. If they ate it, it was a sign of success, but if they ignored it, failure was said to follow.

Mass production of chicken meat and eggs began in the early twentieth century with the invention of the first electrical incubator (later models would even turn the eggs). This increased the number of chickens being bred. The journey towards chickens being kept more for their meat than their eggs began in earnest in 1944 in the USA. That year, the 'Chicken of Tomorrow' contest was launched, where breeders were asked to create a chicken that would grow quickly and produce more edible meat. The winner, announced in 1948, was Charles D. Vantress of California. Agricultural companies quickly seized on the idea, creating proprietary hybrids of different chicken breeds that would need as little food as possible to grow to slaughter-weight. Such birds are also more docile and have lost the browsing instincts the species used to have. This has meant that chickens can be packed together in huge battery farms to maximize profit. Antibiotics are also added to feed, to prevent infectious disease and promote growth. While these innovations have increased output (chickens are now ready for slaughter within six weeks and hens lay over 300 eggs a year) it has come at the cost of the welfare of the chicken.

ELEPHANTS

The largest living land animals, elephants symbolize power, wisdom and authority in cultures across the world. Aside from their size, their most notable feature is their trunk, which is dextrous and sensitive – it can be used to pick up objects, strip trees of vegetation or squirt water. Their tusks, which are enlarged incisors, are used for defence, attacking and digging, while their large ears help dissipate heat from their bodies. There are three species of elephant. The largest is the African bush elephant, which weighs up to 6,000 kilograms (6 tons) and is over 3 metres (around 10 feet) tall at the shoulder. The African forest elephant, recognized as a separate species in 2010, is slightly smaller. The Asian elephant usually weighs around 4,000 kilograms (4 tons) and lives in the Indian subcontinent and South East Asia.

The Indus Valley Civilization, which had arisen by the end of the fourth millennium BC in the northeast of the Indian subcontinent, provides the earliest evidence for human taming of elephants. Seals excavated from their cities depict elephants with cloths over their backs, suggesting they were ridden or used as draught animals. Their intelligence meant that they could be trained, and would form close bonds with their handlers, called mahouts. However, elephants have never been fully domesticated – this is partly because their gestation time of up to twenty-two months (the longest of any mammal) makes selective breeding difficult. They also present a huge logistical difficulty, as they need around 130 kilograms (286 pounds) of food a day.

By the sixth century BC, Indian rulers had realized the military potential of elephants. Capable of speeds of 40 kilometres per hour (25 miles per hour), elephants could wreak havoc, and inflict wounds with their tusks (often tipped with spikes). They also provided a platform for soldiers armed with projectile weapons and allowed commanders to better survey the battlefield. They did not guarantee victory. In 326 BC, Porus, who ruled a kingdom in the Punjab, deployed over one hundred elephants against an invading ruler from the west: Alexander the Great. When they met on the banks of the Hydaspes River, the elephants initially caused great damage among Alexander's infantry before they regrouped and threw javelins at their eyes and hacked at their legs. This caused a problem common with elephants: many panicked and stampeded, making them just as much a threat to their own side as their enemy (for this reason mahouts carried a spike they could use to drive into their mount's brain if they totally lost control). The Greeks won the day, although this marked the eastern limit of Alexander's conquests.

Ancient Rome also faced elephants in battle. This first happened in 280 BC when the Greek king Pyrrhus of Epirus (319/18–272 BC) invaded southern Italy to stop Roman expansion. Initially, he found success with his beasts but the Romans devised tactics to deal with them, notably igniting oil-covered pigs and driving them into the elephants. Their terrified squealing was said to drive the elephants to stampede. Having suffered heavy losses, Pyrrhus was forced to return home in 275 BC.

The Roman Republic's most formidable foe in its rise to becoming the dominant power in the Mediterranean was the Carthaginian Empire, which ruled territory in North Africa, Spain and Sicily. Their first war lasted from 264 to 241 BC and ended with Rome controlling most of Sicily. Conflict restarted in 218 BC with the Carthaginian general Hannibal (247–*c.* 181 BC) invading northern Italy via the Alps. His army included thirty-seven war elephants, which he ambitiously hoped to guide through the high, sometimes narrow, mountain passes. Only six of them survived the trek to descend into Italy and just made it through the following winter. Undeterred, Hannibal won a series of victories against the Romans. He remained in Italy but could not advance on Rome itself and in 204 BC had to return home when the Romans invaded North Africa. There, at the Battle of Zama (202 BC), Hannibal was decisively defeated. When his elephants charged, the Roman lines opened and let them rush through, meaning they could play no major role in the battle. Victorious, Rome then annexed

Spain before winning a final victory over Carthage in 149–146 BC, which led to their capital's destruction and the annexation of all their remaining territory.

JUMBO THE ELEPHANT

Humans have often exploited elephants for entertainment – most famously 'Jumbo'. He was an African bush elephant that was captured in Sudan and brought to London Zoo in 1865, where he became a popular favourite. In 1882, to public outcry, he was sold for £2,000 (over £200,000 today) to the American showman P. T. Barnum (1810–91), who recouped his costs in just two weeks. Jumbo travelled with Barnum's circus until 1885, when he died after being struck by a train in St Thomas in Canada.

Elephants remained prized as weapons of war in the Indian subcontinent, but the advent of effective gunpowder weapons heralded their end; symptomatic of this was the Battle of Panipat in 1526, when the invading Mughal armies defeated the Sultan of Delhi, who had 1,000 war elephants. The Mughal cannons terrified the elephants, who were further panicked by camels loaded with lit straw that were driven into them. After this victory, the Mughals became the dominant power in the Indian subcontinent, and they remained so until the ascendance of the British in the eighteenth and nineteenth centuries. Though not used in battle, armies still made use of elephants as beasts of burden or to assist in military engineering. They were particularly useful in densely forested, tropical conditions, and deployed up to the twentieth century – for example, during World War II the Allies used them to build bridges in the Burmese jungle, while in the Vietnam War the communist North Vietnamese forces used them to carry supplies and equipment.

Trade has caused more damage to elephants than war. Humans have prized elephant ivory, which is durable yet easy to carve, for millennia. By the nineteenth century, demand had reached a peak, as it was made into a huge range of articles including piano keys, snooker balls and buttons. Millions of elephants were slaughtered. As a result, there are now no more than 400,000 African elephants left in the wild and only around 40,000 Asian ones. In both continents, elephants are now protected and there are strict limits placed on the ivory trade, but they still face the problems of poaching and habitat loss. To make matters worse elephants are a 'keystone species', which means they shape ecosystems. Their movement through the landscape creates pathways for other animals, while many plants rely on their seeds being propagated by elephant dung. As such, the loss of elephants would not only lead to the extinction of a majestic animal but also harm other species.

TURTLES

The Chinese writing system is the most widely used in the world, and is among the oldest. It uses thousands of characters to represent both sounds and concepts, and has been a major influence on other writing systems in East Asia, particularly those of Japan and Korea. It dates back to the thirteenth century BC, and one of the first places it was used was on the shells of turtles.

Turtles are a family of 356 species of reptiles whose bodies are encased in a bony (or sometimes cartilaginous) shell. It is an integral part of their body that cannot be shed as their ribs and vertebrae are fused to it. The top part of the shell, the carapace, is joined to the bottom part, the plastron, by bone and cartilage. The majority of turtles are aquatic or semi-aquatic, and live most of their lives in water – their shells are more streamlined and some species have flippers to help them swim. These include the seven species of turtle that live in the sea; they can dive to depths of 900 metres (nearly 3,000 feet) and migrate hundreds of kilometres to specific beaches to lay their eggs, which they bury and then leave. The largest sea turtle (and largest of all turtles) is the leatherback, which weighs up to 900 kilograms (around 2,000 pounds); unlike other members of the family its shell is not hard and bony but flexible and oily. Around one-eighth of turtles live entirely on land. They are known as tortoises and tend to have higher, more domed shells. They include the smallest member of the turtle family, the speckled padloper, which lives in South Africa and is around 8 centimetres (3 inches) long.

Due to their long lifespan and slow movement (on land at least), turtles often symbolize longevity, stability and wisdom. Many cultures feature the myth of a giant turtle (or tortoise) that carries the entire world (or cosmos) on its shell. For example, in Hindu mythology this turtle, who carries the elephants who directly bear the world on their backs, is known as Akupara. Similarly, in Chinese mythology, the creator goddess Nüwa cut the legs off a giant turtle to support the heavens after a destructive water god damaged the mountain that had previously held them up.

The discovery of the origins of Chinese writing goes back to 1899, when Wang Yirong (1845–1900), the president of the Imperial University in Beijing, was unwell. His servant brought him 'dragon bones' as a remedy. They were a popular ingredient in traditional Chinese medicine, ground down into powder to treat wounds and illness. Wang saw there were inscriptions on the bones and ordered his servant to return to the apothecary and purchase the rest of its stock, which amounted to about 300 pieces. News of the potential importance of the bones spread, and scholars and collectors began to purchase and analyse the bones. It became clear they were in fact a mixture of turtle plastrons and the scapula of cattle, and that they were used for divination, meaning they became known as 'oracle bones'.

Oracle bones date back to the Shang dynasty era (*c.* 1600–1046 BC). The Shang arose out of the numerous civilizations that emerged in the Yellow River valley and ruled territory in north and central China. They are the first dynasty for whom there is concrete archaeological evidence. The oracle bones had been dug up close to the city of Anyang in central China. Archaeological work revealed this was the site of Yin, the Shang capital from 1300 BC until the dynasty's overthrow in 1046 BC, after which the city was abandoned. Excavations uncovered thousands of oracle bones there.

Writing in China developed as a way for the Shang kings to ask questions about the future by communicating with Heaven. The shells and bones had to be scraped clean and highly polished before the answers sought during the divination ceremony were inscribed on them (or sometimes written using ink). The writing featured pictographs that would become characteristic of Chinese script. A hot poker was then applied, which created stress cracks across the shell. These would then be interpreted to tell the Shang kings if they should follow a certain course of action (for example, if they should go on a military campaign). Over 150,000 oracle bones have been found, containing 4,500 symbols (not all of which have been deciphered), which help show how Chinese writing developed. The oracle bones also contained important information about major events and figures of the Shang dynasty era.

Today, many turtle species are endangered. This is partly due to demand for their meat, shells and eggs, as well as pollution and climate change. Sea turtles are particularly at risk due to the additional perils of losing shoreline nesting sites, marine debris and being accidentally tangled up in fishing nets. For turtles to survive into the twenty-first century and beyond, their habitats, both terrestrial and maritime, must be respected.

TU'I MALILA

Tortoises are among the longest-living animals in the world. The oldest known is a radiated tortoise from Madagascar that may have lived to 188 years. It is said that Captain James Cook presented it to the Tongan royal family in 1777. Believing it to be a male, it was named Tu'i ('King') Malila but after it died in 1966, examination suggested it may have been female.

THE GUARD GEESE
OF THE CAPITOLINE HILL

. . . .

Before Rome was the capital of an empire that extended
from Britain to Mesopotamia, it was one of many city
states in Central Italy. Just as Rome was emerging as
a regional power, during the early fourth century BC, a
foreign army sacked it for the first time. Though seriously
damaged, the city was delivered from total destruction by
an unlikely saviour: a flock of geese.

Rome was established around the tenth century BC
(the traditional date is 753 BC), and it was initially ruled
by kings before switching over to a republican system in
509 BC. After it became a republic, Rome became the
leading power in its region, Latium, by conquering its
neighbours. As Rome was about to expand further, it faced
a new threat: Gallic tribes invading northern Italy. In
around 390 BC (some accounts place the date three years
later), Rome sent an army to defeat one of the tribes, the
Senones, who were led by their chieftain Brennus. They
met at the Allia River, 16 kilometres (10 miles) northeast of Rome. It was a rout. Thousands of Romans were
slaughtered and survivors sought shelter in Veii, a walled
city Rome had recently captured and occupied. This left

the way clear for Brennus to advance on Rome, which his men sacked. A small garrison who remained in Rome sought refuge on the *Arx*, a citadel atop the Capitoline Hill, which the Senones then besieged.

Late one night the Senones crept up the Capitoline Hill to finish off the Romans. They had eluded both the guards and the watchdogs and were poised to strike down the last bastion of Roman resistance until, according to several ancient accounts, a loud honking broke the silence. They had disturbed a flock of geese kept by the priests at a temple dedicated to Juno, goddess of marriage and childbirth and wife of Jupiter. This woke Marcus Manlius Capitolinus (d. 384 BC), a former consul (the highest elected position in Rome), who struck down a Gaul who had reached the summit. Roused, the rest of the garrison joined him to repulse the attack. Rome had been saved.

It is not impossible that geese would have behaved this way. Geese are not particularly fearful of people, are highly territorial and are known to loudly honk or cry out when danger is near or they are disturbed. They also have excellent hearing and their eyesight is better than a human's. They can even sense ultraviolet, which makes their vision sharper. As such, a flock of geese may well be just as effective a sentry as any human or canine.

After the Senones had been driven off the Capitoline Hill, the siege continued – some sources suggest it lasted seven months. Meanwhile, the Romans outside Rome had regrouped under the leadership of the politician Marcus Furius Camillus (c. 446–365 BC), who had been made dictator (a temporary office, usually awarded in times of military emergency, that gave the holder total power over the state). Eventually, with both sides running low on food and the Senones succumbing to disease, spread because they had not buried the dead, peace negotiations began. The Romans agreed to give Brennus 450 kilograms (1,000 pounds) of gold to lead his army away. Just as payment was about to be made, Camillus arrived and declared the deal was off and that Rome would be regained 'not with gold, but with iron'. Camillus then led his army against the Senones, with fighting taking place amid Rome's ruined streets. The Senones were driven out and then defeated in a pitched battle the next day. Not all historical accounts are this dramatic, and some suggest that the ransom was in fact duly paid, and the Senones withdrew.

Regardless of how the Senones left, Rome was rebuilt within a year. New, better-quality city walls were erected. A new temple to Juno, in her aspect as a giver of warnings and prophecies, was constructed on the Capitoline Hill in 344 BC. Rome's narrow escape from total destruction was memorialized in a ceremony called the *supplicia canum* ('punishment of the dogs'). Every year, dogs were sacrificed and suspended on wooden stakes, while geese were dressed in purple and gold and paraded through the streets in a litter. Rome would go from strength to strength, and by the late third century BC controlled virtually the entire Italian peninsula, before expanding to become the one of the greatest empires in world history. Rome would not be sacked again until AD 410, when Visigoths ransacked the city. By then, Rome was in steady decline, and by the end of the fifth century AD its power in Western Europe had collapsed.

SWANS

Zeus once appeared as a swan to seduce the princess Leda; their child was Helen of Troy. Swans also feature prominently in Norse and Irish mythology and in Hinduism are symbols of wisdom, purity and transcendence.

LLAMAS

. . . .

The Inca Empire was the greatest power to emerge in the New World before the arrival of the Europeans. Expanding beyond its capital city of Cusco in the Andes, it began to conquer neighbouring areas during the early fourteenth century AD. By the early sixteenth century, the Inca controlled territory that extended 4,000 kilometres (2,500 miles) along the western side of South America and ruled a population of 12 million people. It was a highly organized state, with a well-developed administration and infrastructure. A major factor in Inca strength, and other earlier Andean cultures, was the llama, the largest animal to be domesticated in the Americas.

The llama is a member of the camelids, although unlike its distant relative the camel, it does not have a hump. Arising on the Great Plains of North America over 40 million years ago, the ancestors of the llama migrated to South America about 3 million years ago, adjusting to live at the high altitudes of the Andes by having more red blood cells than other animals, increasing the oxygen that can be carried in the bloodstream, as well as a bigger lung capacity.

Over 6,000 years ago, llamas were domesticated from a smaller animal called the guanaco, which still lives in large numbers in the wild. The llama has a number of natural features that make it well suited to act as a pack animal. Extremely social, they live in herds and are content in large groups. They can carry around 35 kilograms (nearly 80 pounds) for up to 30 kilometres (nearly 20 miles) a day. The llama is compliant unless it is overloaded or tired – in which case it might refuse to move or kick or spit. The llama also has a high thirst tolerance and eats a wide range of forage. The Inca also used the llama for other purposes. Its meat was eaten and its fat made into candles. Llama manure was employed as a fertilizer and used to make ceramics and dried as a fuel source. Finally, the llama's wool could be used to make fabrics, as well as rugs and rope.

The alpaca is another camelid species that was domesticated in the Andes at about the same time as the llama. Derived from another species, the vicuña, the alpaca is smaller than the llama, has a more rounded body, and prefers higher altitudes. Rather than serving as a pack animal, it was most valued for its wool, which is strong, lightweight and a superb natural insulator. As such, it was often reserved for making textiles for the elites.

The Inca were not the first Andean civilization to use the llama, but they were certainly the one that used it most extensively. Inca authorities raised and carefully managed large herds of llamas, using them in trains of several hundred to carry trade goods across the network of roads and trails that criss-crossed their empire, linking highland and lowland areas. Every November, they carried out an annual census of llamas, noting them on *quipu*, a system of knotted ropes they used to keep records. They also acted swiftly to prevent outbreaks of disease among llamas – when one fell sick, it was culled and buried to prevent it transmitting the ailment. Inca agriculture was highly developed – they built terraced fields and irrigation systems to grow crops like maize and potatoes; yields were greatly increased thanks to llama dung.

The llama's importance was reflected in many aspects of Inca culture. According to Inca mythology, they originated from three caves near the village of Paqari-tampu (25 kilometres [15 miles] south of Cusco). At the same time as they emerged, so did the llama, reflecting their central status in Inca society. Llamas played an important role in Inca ritual; they were often sacrificed as offerings to the gods, and their mummified remains (as well as small golden figurines of them) were often buried with high-status individuals. The Inca also named one of their most important constellations, the *Yacana*, after the llama, believing it was the source of their energy.

In 1532, the era of Inca greatness came to an end, thanks to the arrival of the Spanish conquistador Francisco Pizarro (*c.* 1471/6–1541) and 168 men. Making up for their numerical disadvantage was their steel weaponry and armour, as well as gunpowder weapons. The Spanish also had the horse. Unlike the llama it could carry a man and was also strong enough to drive machinery or pull wheeled vehicles (although in many ways this was moot as the Inca never developed the wheel). Shortly after arriving, the Spanish inflicted a heavy defeat on the Inca at the Battle of Cajamarca, capturing their emperor. The next year, Pizarro and his men occupied Cusco, effectively ending the Inca Empire and beginning Spanish imperial control of their territory.

Spanish colonization nearly spelled the end of the llama. By the early seventeenth century, its numbers had declined by over 80 per cent as a result of new diseases from Europe, being killed for its meat and losing grazing land to sheep. However, the llama continued to be used by the indigenous population as a beast of burden, preserving the species. By the later twentieth century, the llama had spread outside South America; its sought-after fleeces mean it is now an increasingly popular livestock species in countries like the USA and UK. In addition, llamas have alternative uses including acting as therapy animals and guards to protect livestock from predators.

Homing Pigeons

On 19 September 1870, Prussian forces, together with their German allies, besieged Paris. With the city encircled, attempts at a breakout easily thwarted, and no relief army coming, the people of Paris faced a long, hungry winter. As telegraph cables had been cut, Paris's main link to the outside world was via hot-air balloons bearing mail. Some also carried an animal that had been used for communication for millennia: homing pigeons.

When the birds landed behind the German lines, messages were attached to them by the French to be carried back to their beleaguered capital. The medium was cutting-edge: microfilm, which was recovered from the pigeon and then projected using a magic lantern (an early form of projector), transcribed and delivered. Despite the fact that only one-sixth of the 360 pigeons returned to Paris (the Prussians used guns and hawks to bring them down), over 60,000 messages were still received. The siege ended on 28 January 1871, with German troops marching through Paris, but it was a reminder of the unique talent of the homing pigeon.

The homing pigeon is a domesticated version of the rock dove, which in the wild lives on coastal cliffs and mountains. It has been selectively bred since 3000 BC, and feral versions have adapted to live in towns and cities worldwide. Homing pigeons can find their way back home to their lofts even if released over 900 kilometres (560 miles) away in unfamiliar territory. Strong, powerful flyers, they can reach speeds of around 90 kilometres per hour (over 55 miles per hour). Scientists suggest they find their way by sensing the Earth's magnetic field, but studies have also shown they are able to navigate using remembered landmarks (they have been observed following motorways and turning off at junctions). This meant that homing pigeons were the quickest, and often most reliable, way of sending messages long-distance before the advent of the electrical telegraph during the 1840s.

Following their deployment in the Siege of Paris, governments around Europe built up their stocks of homing pigeons, realizing they could play a vital role in communication during warfare, when telegraph services were likely to be disrupted. When the British did not follow suit quickly enough, this led to fears they may be falling behind. One of the great boosters of closing this 'pigeon gap' was Alfred Osman (1864–1930). He was the owner of a weekly newspaper called *The Racing Pigeon*, which catered to the thousands of people who raised the birds and those who gambled on their races. Soon after World War I broke out in 1914, Osman established the Voluntary Pigeon War Committee. Operating without pay, his first major initiative was to found a network of lofts along England's east coast to allow ships and seaplanes to send notification of enemy naval activity in the North Sea. He then oversaw their deployment on the Western Front, mounting mobile lofts that could hold over sixty homing pigeons on top of converted buses. Although telegraphs connected trenches to headquarters, artillery bombardment often cut them off and prompt repairs were not always possible. Under these conditions homing pigeons could be used by soldiers on the front line, as well as those advancing into no man's land, to send messages to their commanders. They were also carried by tank crews, although the homing pigeons sometimes became confused because of oil fumes. Belgian spies who parachuted behind German lines were issued with homing pigeons in baskets, which were then sent back with reports of enemy positions. By the end of World War I, Osman's organization had over 350 handlers and had distributed 100,000 birds.

At the start of World War II, militaries had access to portable field telephones and radio transceivers. Yet these new technologies were still vulnerable to technical faults, being damaged or having their signals jammed or disrupted. Once again, the British government turned to the homing pigeon. In June 1940, they launched an appeal to encourage pigeon fanciers to volunteer their birds for war service. Their most ambitious use was in Operation Columba, which began on 8 April 1941. It saw the Royal Air Force drop 16,554 homing pigeons across Nazi-occupied Europe, from Denmark to southern France. They were placed inside containers with an envelope and questionnaire for the people who found them to fill in and place inside a cylinder clipped to the pigeon's leg. They were encouraged to send information about German

CHER AMI

During World War I, the Americans had their own pigeon service numbering 6,000 birds, and its most famous member was Cher Ami. On her twelfth mission, on 4 October 1918, she was shot through the chest and leg, blinded in one eye, but returned to her loft. Her message, attached by a single tendon, revealed the position of a battalion that had become isolated and were under heavy fire. They were relieved and 194 men were saved. Cher Ami was fitted with a wooden leg, awarded the French *Croix de Guerre* and returned home to the USA, where she died the next year.

movements and positions, potential targets for bombardment and even if they were hearing broadcasts from the BBC. The messages were vital in helping to shape a picture of the disposition of German forces, particularly prior to the D-Day landings in Normandy. Homing pigeons were also issued to military personnel, particularly flight crews in bombers, who carried them in special watertight containers. They proved to be lifesavers; for example, in 1942, after a British bomber ditched in the North Sea, its crew released their homing pigeon, Winkie, who flew 190 kilometres (nearly 120 miles) to her loft near Dundee. A rescue mission was launched and the crew was found in fifteen minutes. For her service, in 1943, Winkie became one of the first recipients of the Dickin Medal, established to recognize the gallantry of animals serving with military and civil defence units. Over the course of World War II, thirty-one more homing pigeons would be similarly honoured. Homing pigeons are still bred, highly prized by fanciers and competitively raced, but they have been rendered obsolete as a form of communication.

EMUS

. . . .

Countless species have been the subject of violence at the hands of humans. In 1932, this escalated into direct armed conflict, when the Australian Army attempted to eliminate thousands of emus in one of the most unusual 'wars' in military history.

Australia has been separate from other continents for over 35 million years, meaning it has developed some of the most unique animals on Earth, including the kangaroo, quokka, echidna, koala and Tasmanian devil. Also native to Australia is the emu, the second-largest living bird. Between 1.5 and 1.8 metres (5 to 6 feet) tall and weighing up to 45 kilograms (100 pounds), it is flightless, with relatively small, 20-centimetre-long (8 inches) wings. The emu makes up for this with its running ability, and can reach speeds of around 50 kilometres per hour (30 miles per hour). Travelling across the Australian landscape in 'mobs' of thousands, it forages on fruits, seeds, shoots and small animals.

Humans arrived in Australia over 50,000 years ago, crossing from South East Asia. The Aboriginal Australians settled across the continent, establishing the world's oldest continuous civilization. For the most part, they lived as nomadic hunter-gatherers, although some groups practised forms of agriculture. Emus were one of their food sources (their bones, feathers, fat and tendons were also put to use), and they would attract them by imitating their calls, netting them or poisoning their watering holes. Their large green-shelled eggs, which weighed over 400 grams (14 ounces), were also a useful source of protein. As was common in hunter-gatherer society, there was little population growth, and by the late eighteenth century perhaps only 300,000 people lived in Australia.

This changed in 1788, when a British fleet carrying over 1,000 people arrived at Botany Bay aiming to establish a penal colony. Europeans had travelled to Australia before, starting with the Dutch navigator Willem Janszoon (c. 1570–c. 1630), but this would be the first permanent settlement. This 'First Fleet' signalled mass European colonization of Australia; millions more migrants would follow, spreading out across the continent. Any property rights the Aboriginal Australians had were ignored, as the British declared the land *terra nullis*, that is, vacant and belonging to no one. There were thousands of Aboriginal deaths at the hands of settler violence and novel diseases they had no natural immunity to. European colonization also harmed native flora and fauna by introducing new animal species, such as cats, foxes, rabbits and pigs. Most damaging was the poisonous cane toad, introduced from Hawaii in 1935 to control the cane beetle, which was damaging sugar cane crops. From a population of 2,400 released in northern Queensland, cane toads have increased their range by around 2,000 kilometres, and now number over 200 million. They have been damaging to native species, causing some local extinctions.

In 1901, the Commonwealth of Australia was created by federating six British self-governing colonies. During World War I, when over 400,000 Australians enlisted in the military, the government established a scheme to grant servicemen land after demobilization (Aboriginal Australian veterans were not eligible, however). Many veterans were given land in Western Australia, which, at over 2.5 million square kilometres (around 1 million square miles) in size, was the largest state but also sparsely populated. They were encouraged to grow wheat, which the government offered to subsidize. By 1932, these farmers were in dire straits: the world was mired in the Great Depression, subsidies were unpaid and there was a drought. To make matters worse, in the district around the town of Campion, a mob of 20,000 emus arrived. They tore down fences, trampled the wheat crop and ate even the smallest shoots, putting the harvest of the entire region in peril. Desperate farmers lobbied the federal government in Canberra for assistance.

Help arrived in the form of Major G. P. W. Meredith of the Seventh Heavy Battery of the Royal Australian Artillery, who led two soldiers. They were armed with two Lewis machine guns (capable of firing 500 rounds per minute) and 10,000 rounds of ammunition. Also accompanying the military expedition was a camera operator to film it, as the federal government wanted to publicize its support for the farmers. Meredith and his men arrived in early October but rains scattered the emus, meaning the operations against them were postponed until the next month. On 2 November, Meredith and his two men camped outside Campion. When fifty emus approached their position, Meredith asked local farmers

Ostriches

The world's largest living bird is the ostrich, which grows up to 2.7 metres (nearly 9 feet) and can reach weights of 160 kilograms (over 350 pounds). They are faster than the emu and can get up to 70 kilometres per hour (43 miles per hour) when sprinting. Their eyes, which are around 5 centimetres (2 inches) across, are the biggest of any land animal.

to flank them and drive them towards his firing line. Instead, the emus ran out of range, meaning they only suffered limited casualties. Two days later, Meredith tried a different tactic – he ambushed a group of emus near a watering hole but could only kill a few dozen because they scattered too quickly. To try to pursue the emus, Meredith mounted his machine guns on a truck. The rough terrain meant the emus easily outran them and also made aiming impossible. By 8 November, Meredith had only killed 200 emus and was recalled. At the request of the farmers, he returned on 13 November, but after a week still could not inflict heavy casualties. The soldiers reported that the emu was incredibly difficult to kill, with only a head shot guaranteed to bring them down. Meredith claimed he had killed 1,000 emus in total but the toll was probably far lower, and they remained a nuisance in the area. It appeared that the emus had won this 'war'. In the long run, the emus were controlled by giving farmers bullets and offering them a bounty, as well as improvements to fences. Emus and humans appear to have come to a detente. Western Australia has become one of the most important grain-producing regions in the world and the national emu population numbers over 700,000.

3

LEGEND, RELIGION AND SYMBOLISM

CATS

. . . .

The smallest member of the *Felidae* family, which consists of thirty-seven species including the tiger, cheetah and lion, is the cat. They have lived with humans for around 9,500 years, and were first domesticated in West Asia. By this time, the Agricultural Revolution, which began in Mesopotamia, had led to the establishment of farming villages in the region, which attracted small rodents and birds seeking food amid the fields and granaries. This provided a food source for carnivorous wildcats, who began to live in and around these settlements. Over the generations, they gradually became domesticated, growing closer to humans and eventually moving into their homes, although they retained the sharp hunting instincts of their wild ancestor. Cats remain the ideal creature for vermin control. They have strong senses of smell, hearing and vision, are agile and well balanced, and have sharp, retractable claws. From West Asia, cats spread across Eurasia and Africa. Cats were independently domesticated in central China from the wild leopard cat around 3300 BC. Bones excavated from farming villages suggest they consumed small grain-eating rodents, but this domesticated version of the leopard cat had disappeared within three centuries.

No civilization has venerated cats as much as ancient Egypt, where they first began to be kept over 6,000 years ago. In the mid-third millennium BC, cats were declared a sacred animal, and they became the subject of worship. Bronze models of cats were used as offerings, and figurines of them were worn as protective amulets. In the city of Bubastis, a cult of the cat-headed goddess Bastet, the daughter of the sun-god Ra, emerged. Bastet had begun as a warlike lioness goddess, but as she became more associated with the cat she became gentler and a patron of pregnancy and childbirth, as well as a protector against evil spirits and disease. There was an extensive temple devoted to her at Bubastis, where thousands of mummified cats have been found. When a family's cat died it was commonplace to mummify them, and they were often buried next to their masters (often with mummified mice for the afterlife). Indeed, the death of a cat was the cause of great mourning in Egypt. Causing them harm was considered a taboo, and by the mid-fifth century BC, killing them was punished by death.

In a mostly arid region, Egypt thrived thanks to the waters provided by the Nile, whose annual flooding helped make the soil fertile. Food-stores were the foundation of wealth and prestige; as cats protected them so efficiently against the depredations of vermin, it is little wonder the ancient Egyptians held them in such high esteem. Eventually, it would be to their detriment, and helped speed the fall of the Egyptian pharaohs. In 525 BC, the Persian Empire, led by Cambyses II (d. 522 BC), invaded Egypt. His army approached Pelusium, an important city on the eastern Nile Delta. One ancient source suggests the Persian soldiers drove cats before them, held them in their arms and painted images of them on their shields. This made the Egyptians reluctant to fight them, leading to the Persians achieving a decisive victory. They then conquered the capital, Memphis, and made Egypt a Persian province. After this, Egypt was directly ruled or dominated by a series of external powers (including the Greeks, Romans,

Byzantines, Arabs, Ottomans and British) before winning independence as a republic in 1953.

Crimean Tom

On 9 September 1855, during the Crimean War, Anglo-French forces captured the Russian fortress city of Sevastopol after a punishing eleven-month siege. While foraging for supplies in the devastated city, a British officer noticed a cat amid the rubble, who he adopted and named Tom. Tom then sniffed out food caches in the ruins, helping save British and French soldiers from starvation. He was later taken to England, where he died in 1856.

Despite the pharaoh forbidding their export, from around 1500 BC domesticated cats spread from Egypt into Europe. They were carried along trade routes, initially by the Phoenicians. A maritime people who originated from modern-day Lebanon, they established a commercial empire along the ancient Mediterranean coast. The Phoenicians probably carried cats on board their ships to control vermin there, something they were as adept at doing at sea as they were on land. Later, from the sixteenth to nineteenth centuries AD, cats would be similarly spread by European ships to the Americas, Australia and elsewhere, often to the detriment of local wildlife who proved easy pickings to the new arrivals. Indeed, cats have caused the extinction of at least thirty-three species, and kill billions of birds and small mammals every year.

If ancient Egypt was the apogee of cat adoration, then medieval Europe was their nadir. Among many Christians, cats, particularly black ones, came to be seen as a malevolent force and a representation of evil. Those in league with the Devil, such as witches, were said to use cats as their 'familiars' (animals they would use to do their evil bidding), and they were sometimes associated with heretical groups. During the Black Death (1346–53), cats often bore the brunt of the blame for spreading the disease, and thousands of them were killed. Cats were more positively viewed in East Asia, where they were seen as bringing good fortune. In Japan, the *Maneki-neko* ('beckoning cat') figurine has become a popular lucky talisman in many homes and businesses, referencing a legend in which a cat saved an emperor from being struck by lightning by beckoning him inside into a temple. However, in Thailand (once known as Siam) cats were even more beloved as symbols of domesticity and prosperity. Cats held a special status among the royal family, which kept and bred them, meaning that Thailand is home to many of the most cherished and historical breeds, including the Siamese and the Khao Manee (which means 'white gem').

Fortunately for cats (and their human owners), by the nineteenth century the negative perception of cats in the West had dwindled. They are now among the most popular pets in the world and a beloved member of millions of households.

EURASIAN BROWN BEARS

Many cultures regard bears with awe, love and respect. There are eight species of bear; they are generally good climbers and swimmers, with an excellent sense of smell, a strong bite and an inquisitive nature. With the exception of the spectacled bears of the Andes, they all live in the northern hemisphere. Their habitats range from the Arctic Circle, where the polar bear roams, to the tropical forests of South East Asia that are home to the sun bear. The vast majority of bears live in forests. The most widespread is the brown bear, which ranges from Spain across Eurasia to northern Japan. A subspecies of brown bear, known as the grizzly, lives in North America.

Animism, the concept that plants, animals, inanimate objects and features of the landscape can be imbued with some form of spiritual essence, occurs in systems of religious beliefs around the world. In these cultures there is frequently no strict delineation between the physical world and the spiritual one, making it possible to move between the two planes of existence. Following the rise of Christianity and, subsequently, Islam, such religions were frequently characterized as 'pagan', and subjected to suppression through persecution and forced conversion, leading to their decline. Despite this, pagan and animist customs and beliefs took centuries to fully dislodge and often tenaciously clung on in many areas, particularly remote, rural ones. Given the brown bear's powerful and indomitable nature, many 'pagan' peoples have placed it at the centre of their spiritual world, even regarding it as an ancestral or guiding spirit.

Before they were Christianized during the twelfth and thirteenth centuries, the pagan Finns considered the brown bear a sacred animal and a guardian of the forest (it is now one of Finland's national animals). Central to this was a celebration called the Karhunpeijaiset, where the bear was ritually killed. It was then brought back to the village for a great feast, where its meat was divided and its teeth given out to wear as amulets. It was believed this would imbue people with the bear's senses and powers. After the feast, the bear's skull and bones were carried back to the forest in a procession, accompanied by songs. The skull was hung from a tree, while the bones were buried. This ritual partly showed respect for the bear but also showed man's mastery over nature.

Siberia's indigenous peoples regarded the brown bear with similar respect. For example, the Evenks believed the bear was the creator of the world, and had been responsible for giving people the gift of fire.

Many viewed the bear as an earthly manifestation of their ancestors, calling it 'grandfather' or 'father'. To express this veneration, the Nivkh peoples performed a ceremony where they captured a bear cub and raised it as a member of the village. It would then be dressed in a ceremonial costume and slaughtered, symbolizing its return to the spirit world, with the hope it would deliver blessings in the future. This, and similar rituals among other peoples of Siberia, continued even after the onset of Communist rule, where there were attempts to ban them as outdated superstitions. Although worship of the brown bear was frowned upon, it remained a long-lasting symbol of the Russian nation before, during and after the Communist era.

Hokkaido is the northernmost of Japan's five main islands. Its indigenous people are the Ainu, who settled it over 20,000 years ago, arriving from Siberia via a land bridge. The Ainu were hunter-gatherers and farmers. They maintained a society largely distinct from the rest of Japan. This remained the case until the sixteenth century AD, when Japanese rulers began extending their power north and claimed control of Hokkaido. Many Japanese settled Hokkaido, and the Ainu population declined as a result of violence and disease. Despite this, the Ainu culture and language clung on, and knowledge of Ainu

GIANT PANDAS

The giant panda of South Central China, the only herbivorous bear, is an iconic species, possibly because of its striking black and white fur. The black parts help it hide in the shadows of the forest, while the white parts act as camouflage in the snow. The black patches around their eyes have a unique size and shape for each panda, helping them recognize each other.

customs has survived. One of the best known involved the brown bear. Like many indigenous Siberians, the Ainu regarded it as a kindred spirit, partly because they shared an omnivorous diet of fish and berries. To them, the bear was a divine being that was visiting the world in the flesh and fur of the bear. In a ceremony called the *iyomante*, a bear cub would be adopted during the winter. It would then be raised as a member of the village, fed with human food, and sometimes even suckled by women. After two or three years, it would be sacrificed by being shot with arrows then strangled and beheaded. This would free its spirit to return to the heavens, although it would of course leave its fur and pelt to the people. Three days of feasting, dancing and singing followed the sacrifice. The brown bear thus served to nourish the community as well as reminding it of their strong ties to the natural world.

GREY WOLVES

Living across Eurasia and North America, the grey wolf, known simply as the 'wolf', is highly adaptive, capable of surviving in deserts, forests and Arctic tundra. They were once even more widely dispersed, living as far afield as Japan, Mexico and southern China. Although the grey wolf is not native to Africa, there is a related species, the Ethiopian wolf, which lives in that continent. Until recently classified as a type of jackal, it lives in the Ethiopian Highlands and is an endangered species.

Figuring prominently in the mythos of many cultures, wolves range from being fierce antagonists to courageous ancestors. It is unsurprising that many peoples have admired them. Wolves are indefatigable hunters, usually travelling at least 20 kilometres (over 12 miles) a day and reaching speeds of nearly 65 kilometres per hour (40 miles per hour). Perhaps the reason wolves are so esteemed is their pack structure, a byword for loyalty and togetherness. Wolves live in strongly bonded and territorial groups of six to ten, usually consisting of an 'alpha' mated pair and their offspring. After reaching sexual maturity, offspring may spend time as a 'lone wolf' before joining or forming another pack. Larger packs, of around forty, have been observed, but these tend to exist only on a temporary basis. The pack works together in search of food, communicating through scent-marking, body language and howling. Through cooperation, they can bring down much larger animals, such as musk oxen, moose or bears.

Most destructive of mythical wolves is Fenrir, who appears in Norse and Germanic folklore. The child of the trickster god Loki and a giantess, Fenrir grew to such ferocity and size that the gods had to bind him to the ground with chains and gag him with a sword. Yet, it was foretold that on *Ragnarök*, the end of the present world, Fenrir will break free and devour the sun. This theme of animalistic loss of control formed part of the popular belief in werewolves in late medieval and early modern Europe. Either through a malevolent curse or a bite, some people would transform into wolves (or a form of man-wolf hybrid), usually every full moon, causing chaos and bloodshed. In the midst of the European witch craze, which saw thousands of innocent people (the vast majority of whom were women) subjected to violence and persecution, a few were also tried and executed for being werewolves, most famously Peter Stumpp (d. 1589), a German farmer found guilty of killing eighteen people. Stumpp claimed the Devil had given him a belt that gave him the ability to shape-shift into a wolf. Just as witch trials had largely declined by the mid-eighteenth century, so had suspected cases of werewolves, although both remained a powerful and lasting trope in popular culture.

Wolves are intrinsically bound up in the mythos of two of the greatest empires in world history. The legendary founder of Rome is Romulus, offspring of the god Mars and Rhea Silvia, a princess from Alba Longa, a city state in central Italy. As infants, Romulus and his twin brother, Remus, were sentenced to death by their great uncle Amulius, who had seized the throne of Alba Longa and wanted to eliminate any potential rival. Amulius's servants, unwilling to have blood on their hands, tried to kill the twins by exposure, placing them in a basket and letting it drift along the River Tiber. Romulus and Remus were discovered by a she-wolf, who brought them to her den and suckled them, while a woodpecker brought them food. They were later found and raised by a shepherd and his wife. As adults, Romulus and Remus founded a city together on the seven hills overlooking the Tiber. After they could not agree on a site, Romulus began to mark out the position of walls around the Palatine Hill. When Remus sarcastically jumped over them to show his disdain, Romulus killed him (other accounts suggest the gods struck him dead for his mockery). Romulus then became the first king of Rome, overseeing its establishment and initial growth. The image of the she-wolf and twins became an important part of Roman iconography as it grew into an imperial power.

The wolf is also central to the Mongol Empire. Its founder, Genghis Khan (1162–1227), claimed descent from a mythical blue-grey wolf said to be the common ancestor of the Mongol people. After unifying the various Mongol clans in 1206, Genghis laid the foundation of an empire that eventually extended from Korea to Central Europe. An occasional ally of the Mongols in their campaigns were the Turkic peoples, who were also nomads from the Eurasian Steppe. They would eventually become a force in their own right, and conquer and rule territories in Central Asia and Anatolia. One of these territories would become the Ottoman Empire, which would eventually spread over three continents, ruling much of North Africa, south-eastern Europe and the Middle East. An important part of Turkic mythology was the she-wolf Asena. She was said to have rescued and raised a Turkic prince who was the sole survivor of his people after a brutal war. Together, Asena and the prince had ten human-wolf children, who were the ancestors of the Turkic peoples.

For all of the respect it is paid, the wolf's predatory instinct has often placed it at odds with mankind. Although wolf attacks on humans are rare, in many areas they were a direct competitor for meat. Moreover, their attacks on livestock in particular have made them a threat to the prosperity, and sometimes even survival, of some communities. Wolves became viewed as vermin and were hunted and killed indiscriminately by farmers and ranchers, which by the mid-twentieth century had brought them to the point of extinction in North America and Europe. Conservation efforts in the past half-century have led to a resurgence in their numbers, to the occasional chagrin of agricultural communities who still regard them as a threat to their livelihood.

PETER THE WILD BOY (C. 1713–85)

Children raised by wild animals are a recurrent trope. There are also historical examples, such as 'Peter', a feral child discovered in 1725 living in the forests of northern Germany. As he could not speak and walked on all fours, many claimed he had been cared for by wolves. He was brought to George I's (1660–1727) court in London, where all attempts to educate him failed. Peter was eventually sent to live on a farm in Hertfordshire, where he died. It is now suspected he had Pitt-Hopkins syndrome, a rare genetic disorder that causes intellectual disability.

Monkeys

. . . .

Monkeys, of which there are nearly 200 species, are primates. They are distinguished from apes by having tails. Most monkeys live in tropical forests, moving from tree to tree, and often using their prehensile tails as an additional limb. They are among the most intelligent and curious animals, and are capable of problem-solving and learning from experience. Highly social, they mostly live in troops, often numbering into the hundreds, usually led by females.

There are two groups of monkeys: Old World and New World. Old World monkeys are native to Africa and Asia (albeit with one small European population in Gibraltar), while their New World cousins live in South and Central America. Due to their inquisitiveness and occasional mischievousness, monkeys often appear in folklore as clever, irrepressible tricksters (although in the Maya religion the howler monkey god is a patron of the arts and artisanship), none more so than two of the most beloved figures of East Asian legend: Hanuman and Sun Wukong.

The *Ramayana*, composed during the fourth century BC, is an epic Sanskrit poem. It tells the story of Rama, the seventh avatar of Vishnu, one of the principal Hindu deities. One of Rama's chief companions was the monkey Hanuman. Possessed of magical abilities, Hanuman's youthful misdeeds led a sage into cursing him to forget them. When the demon king Ravana kidnapped Rama's wife Sita and took her across the sea to his island fortress of Lanka, Hanuman was instrumental in getting her back. After being reminded of his gifts, Hanuman grew to giant size and sprang to Lanka in a single leap, exploring the island and finding out where Sita was imprisoned. He was captured and had his tail set alight but broke free and bounded around Ravana's fortress, creating a great fire. He then returned to Rama and raised a monkey army for him, before building a floating bridge to Lanka. In the ensuing battle that saw Rama defeat Ravana, Hanuman was instrumental, acting as a general and skilfully wielding his *gada* (a spiked mace). When Rama's brother Lakshmana was mortally wounded, Hanuman leapt to a Himalayan mountain because it was the only source of the herbs that would heal him. Unable to find the desired herbs, he used his immense strength to uproot the entire mountain and then delivered it back to the battlefield in time to save Lakshmana. For his devoted service, Rama blessed Hanuman with immortality. There are temples devoted to him across India, and during the seventeenth century he became a symbol of Hindu resistance to the

Muslim Mughal Empire. Hanuman's story spread across Asia; he also appears in Buddhist texts, as well as legends from as far afield as Indonesia, Malaysia and Cambodia.

Hanuman's story spread into China, where it helped inspire Sun Wukong. He first appeared in the novel *Journey to the West*, which was written by Wu Cheng'en (*c.* 1500–82) and is considered one of the classics of Chinese literature. It tells the story of Xuanzang (based on a real figure who lived in the seventh century AD), a Chinese Buddhist monk who travelled to Central Asia and India in search of sacred texts. His protector on the perilous journey would be Sun Wukong. Up to this point, Sun Wukong had lived a chaotic and self-centred

THE MONKEY THAT KILLED A KING

On 2 October 1920, Alexander of Greece (1893–1920) was strolling through Tatoi, his estate north of Athens. Crowned three years previously, he had been reduced to a puppet ruler and had only just returned to the country after scandalously marrying a commoner. That day, he intervened when his German shepherd dog, Fritz, got into an altercation with a Barbary macaque (a breed of monkey native to North Africa) belonging to one of his staff. As Alexander sought to separate the animals, a second Barbary macaque bit him twice. Despite being cleaned, the wounds became infected and he developed sepsis, which killed him on 25 October. His death led to a constitutional crisis, with disputes over the succession and calls for Greece to become a republic. At the time, Greece was engaged in a war with Turkey, and the political upheaval may have contributed to them losing their recent conquests in Anatolia and eventual defeat in 1922.

life. Born from a stone egg, he had immense powers and declared himself the 'Monkey King'. Sun Wukong was able to travel halfway around the world in a single leap, could shape-shift into seventy-two different animals and objects, and was a skilled fighter, wielding a magical golden-banded staff that he could shrink to the size of a needle. When Sun Wukong died he descended into the underworld, where he made himself immortal by erasing his name from the register of life and death. Hearing of his powers, the Jade Emperor, head of the pantheon of traditional Chinese gods, summoned Sun Wukong to Heaven to serve him at his court. Expecting a prestigious post, Sun Wukong flew into a rage when he was merely put in charge of the stables, and eventually violently rebelled against the Jade Emperor, defeating thousands of celestial warriors sent to defeat him. It took the Buddha himself to subdue Sun Wukong; he trapped him under a mountain. After 500 years of imprisonment, Sun Wukong was freed and given the chance to atone for his behaviour by serving Xuanrong. To ensure his good behaviour, Sun Wukong was made to wear an iron headband that painfully tightened if Xuanrong repeated a certain mantra. Sun Wukong proved to be a loyal servant, protecting Xuanrong from thieves and demons and ensuring his safe return to China from the west. For his deeds, Sun Wukong was awarded the title 'Victorious Fighting Buddha'. He had changed radically from the obstreperous figure who treated the world with scorn; his name, which means 'monkey awakened by the emptiness', reflects his journey to enlightenment.

OWLS

Just as the city of Athens came to represent the apogee of ancient Greek cultural influence and intellectual achievement, so too does the owl often stand for knowledge. The two are linked through the goddess Athena, the daughter of Zeus and goddess of wisdom, military strategy and handicraft, and the patron of Athens. Her main symbol is the owl, specifically a species called the little owl. Athena was often depicted with an owl at her side, and it was said to be one of the sources of her wisdom. Although popular across the Hellenic world, Athena was most closely tied to Athens and was probably named after the city. Indeed, the Parthenon, the temple that overlooks Athens and is its chief landmark, is dedicated to her. As a symbol of their allegiance and devotion to Athena, the Athenians declared owls sacred and placed images of them on their coins. When the Athenian phalanx marched into battle, spotting an owl flying overhead was said to presage victory.

There are 225 species of owl, living in every continent except Antarctica and in habitats ranging from tropical forests to frozen tundra. They are all predators, usually of small mammals (although some owls, for example the Eurasian eagle owl, target larger prey such as foxes or occasionally even deer), and are generally nocturnal. Even among birds, none of the species of owl stand out as being particularly intelligent and they are not particularly social, mostly living solitary lives. Owls have small brains compared to their size, tend not to display much inquisitiveness and, unlike many other birds of prey, are difficult to train. Furthermore, whereas many birds are able to construct elaborate nests, owls tend to either steal theirs or use a hollow in a tree or the ground. What the owl may lack in intellect it more than makes up for in its anatomy, which is perfectly calibrated to its needs as a hunter.

The owl's most distinctive feature is its large, wide, forward-facing eyes. It is this that has made many cultures use owls as a representation of wisdom, as it lends them a solemn and distinguished air. These eyes do not actually indicate intelligence but they do give owls incredibly strong vision, particularly in low-light conditions. To achieve this, owls' eyes are disproportionately large compared to the size of their skulls, but they cannot move them in their sockets. To compensate for this, they have the ability to rotate their neck over 270 degrees, meaning they can look behind themselves without moving the rest of their bodies. Owls also have strong hearing; their ears are surrounded by ruffs of feathers to concentrate sound. Their hearing is so precise that they can pinpoint the location of unseen prey just by the sound it makes. This combination of strong sight and hearing makes up for the fact that owls have a poorly developed sense of smell (as well as taste – although this does allow them to eat malodorous species like the skunk). In addition, owls fly in near silence, thanks to feathers that muffle the sound of their wing beats. This means owls hunt by patiently waiting on a perch until they have located a target. Once they do, they can swoop down and pick up their prey from long vegetation or, in the case of some species, fish from the water. These qualities of patience and vision may be the reason that Lakshmi, the Hindu goddess of wealth and good fortune, rides a white owl.

As owls can see in the dark, and see what other animals cannot, they have frequently been viewed as harbingers of future events. Although the ancient Greeks generally believed they were a positive sign, most other peoples did not. This may be connected to their eerie, somewhat other-worldly hooting and screeching. In medieval and early modern England, the call of an owl would presage cold weather or a storm, and their bodies were sometimes nailed to barn doors to protect against lightning. The ancient Romans believed that hearing an owl hooting was an evil omen, while the Apache of the Southwestern United States believe dreaming of an owl was a sign that death is near. Likewise, the Kikuyu people of Central Kenya believed seeing an owl was a sign of death, while the Aztecs linked owls to mortality, and Mictlantecuhtli, their god of the dead, wore their feathers in his headdress and was sometimes depicted with them. Finally, in some parts of India, owls are signs of neither wisdom nor prophesy, but of foolishness, pomposity and laziness.

Clever Crows

The crow group of birds (including ravens, which are larger) are more deserving than owls of being the representation of wisdom. Crows are highly intelligent, skilful mimics and work together to hunt, scavenge and forage. Perhaps the reason they are not as revered as the owl is their habit of purloining shiny objects from humans, leading to a reputation as a pest and trickster.

Eagles

. . . .

Few animals symbolize strength and prestige as much as eagles. Since ancient times, they have stood for might and victory, as well as being associated with divinity. There are over sixty extant species of eagle worldwide. Most eat small mammals, although some have been known to prey on larger targets such as deer, wolves or anteaters, while others focus on snakes and fish. Ultimately, eagles are opportunistic feeders who eat a range of animals, even scavenging carrion and stealing from other predators.

Eagles are important symbols in many religions and often have close links with powerful deities. They are held sacred by many Native American peoples, often seen as linking the earthly and spirit worlds. Their feathers carry a huge amount of prestige, were often awarded to the bravest warriors and continue to be used and worn in ceremonies. The eagle was the companion of the ancient Greek god Zeus, as well as his Roman equivalent, Jupiter. Similarly, the mount of Vishnu, one of the principal Hindu gods, is Garuda, a giant eagle-like being. Eagle-shaped lecterns are used in churches, representing the Word of God being spread (they are also associated with St John the Evangelist, who wrote one of the gospels). For all their spiritual significance, eagles are most associated with the secular world.

The main reason the eagle has been chosen by so many polities to project an image of authority is its association with the Roman Republic and, latterly, the Empire. The foundation of Rome's strength was its military. Rome developed a professional standing army that was organized around a unit called the legion, which numbered between 4,000 and 6,000. One soldier in each legion was charged with carrying the unit's standard, a banner suspended on a long pole, which served as a rallying point and was used to communicate orders. Originally, these standards had been topped by different animals (including wolves, horses or boars) but military reforms enacted in 104 BC specified that only the eagle should be used. Being named *aquilifer* (the soldier who bore the standard) was a high honour and losing their eagle would bring disgrace on the entire legion. The eagle also appeared on coins, sculptures and carvings, acting as one of the Roman Empire's defining symbols.

As a result of internal disorder, economic depression and external invasions (among other factors), Roman power declined during the fourth and fifth centuries. By the time the final emperor in Italy was overthrown in AD 476 by invading Germanic tribes, Roman power in the West had dwindled away. Many rulers with imperial aspirations cloaked themselves in Rome's mantle. One was Charlemagne (AD 748–814), the Frankish king who united much of Western and Central Europe in the early ninth century. In 800, the Pope crowned him 'Holy Roman Emperor', signifying that he was the inheritor of Rome's imperial status. Although Charlemagne's empire fragmented after his death, his legacy remained significant and one of his personal emblems, the eagle, became particularly important in Germany. After Charlemagne's death, the German lands fragmented into hundreds of different states. They, and some surrounding areas, remained part of the Holy Roman Empire, which lasted until 1806, although in practice it was a highly decentralized polity with its constituent states enjoying a high degree of independence. One of them was Prussia, which began as a small duchy in the Baltic region and used the eagle on its coat of arms. Prussia rose to become the dominant force in the reunified German Empire, established in 1871. Its national symbol, which had become synonymous with German unity, was the *Reichsadler* ('Imperial Eagle'). After defeat in World War I, the German Empire was disestablished in 1918, but the eagle remained a national symbol during the Weimar Republic (1918–33) and under Nazi rule (1933–45). When Germany was partitioned in 1949, the eagle was discontinued in the Communist east but following reunification in 1990 it once again became the symbol of the entire country.

The Roman Empire continued in the East as Byzantium. By the thirteenth century, Byzantine emperors had begun to adopt the double-headed eagle as their emblem. It may have originated as a mythical beast from Central Asia, introduced to the Byzantine world by Turkic peoples who migrated to Anatolia. The Byzantine Empire collapsed in 1453, when Ottoman armies captured Constantinople, which they renamed Istanbul. The double-headed eagle continued to be used by two other powers: Russia and the Habsburg dynasty. In both cases, it represented their ambitions to spread their dominions east and west. Both were successful. The Habsburgs established an empire in Central and Eastern Europe that survived until 1918 (the Spanish branch of the family ruled a global empire that extended across South and Central America and into the Philippines). Russia became one of Europe's great powers, expanding into Central Asia and eastward to the Pacific. Communist rule, brought about by the Russian Revolution of 1917, saw the double-headed eagle removed as a symbol of state, but, following the collapse of the Soviet Union, it was reintroduced as the main feature of the national coat of arms in 1993.

The eagle is an important symbol in the Arab world. This is based on its use as a personal standard (in two-headed form) by Salah ad-Din Yusuf (1137–93), better known in the West as Saladin. Saladin, who was actually Kurdish, was one of the great leaders of the medieval world, rising to rule

much of the Middle East. Under his leadership, Crusader control of Jerusalem and the Holy Land, established in 1099, was dealt a terminal blow. The Crusader states did reclaim some territory in the Holy Land (including Jerusalem from 1229 to 1244), but their power was much diminished and they were definitively forced out in 1291. Saladin's eagle re-emerged in 1952, when a group of army officers overthrew the Egyptian monarchy and used it as the symbol of the republic they established. This was fitting, as Cairo had been Saladin's capital. This eagle went on to become an important symbol of Arab nationalism and unity, still featuring on Egypt's coat of arms, as well as those of Iraq, Palestine and Yemen. Another bird of prey, the

Hawk of Quraish (which was the symbol of the Prophet Muhammad's tribe), has been adopted as an emblem by several other Arab nations, including Kuwait, Libya, Syria and the United Arab Emirates.

THE ZIMBABWE BIRD

Built between the eleventh and fifteenth centuries AD, Great Zimbabwe was capital of the Kingdom of Zimbabwe, a powerful polity in southern Africa at that time. After c. 1500, Great Zimbabwe was abandoned; found amid its ruins were soapstone sculptures of eagles. The modern Republic of Zimbabwe, which won independence in 1980, is named after the medieval kingdom, and the sculptures are its national emblem.

Two North American nations, Mexico and the United States, use the eagle as a national symbol. In Mexico, the eagle has been used on the national flag since independence from Spain was won in 1821. The emblem goes back to c. 1325, when the Mexica people, obeying a legendary prophesy, founded the city of Tenochtitlan on the spot where they saw a golden eagle atop a cactus eating a snake. Tenochtitlan went on to become the capital of the Aztec Empire and under Spanish imperial rule the site of Mexico City. Finally, the eagle, specifically the bald eagle, has appeared on the main national symbol of the United States since 1782. Clutching an olive branch of peace in one set of talons and a bundle of thirteen arrows (representing the original number of states) in the other, the eagle has come to stand for American power and prestige, in a sense continuing a legacy of dominion that extends back to Rome.

RED FOXES

The *Vulpes*, also known as the 'true foxes', are a subfamily of the canines. They are smaller than their cousins the wolves and the jackals, and have a flatter skull and black triangular markings between their eyes. The tip of their tail is a different colour to the rest of their body. There are a dozen species of fox, spread across every continent bar Antarctica. They range from the Arctic fox, which can live in temperatures as low as minus 50 degrees Celsius, to the fennec fox, which lives in the arid deserts of North Africa and has large, 15-centimetre (6-inch) ears to radiate body heat. The largest and most widely spread of the *Vulpes* is the red fox, which lives across the northern hemisphere as well as in Australia, where it was introduced during the 1830s, becoming an invasive species. It is able to adapt to living in a wide range of habitats, and its ingenuity has made it a symbol of animal cunning.

One of the great tricksters in European folklore is Reynard the Fox, the protagonist of a series of fables that first appeared in France, Germany and the Low Countries during the twelfth century AD. Although he can be devious and self-centred, often taking advantage of other anthropomorphic animals, particularly his antagonistic uncle Ysengrimus the Wolf, Reynard's stories also show how quick wits can triumph over brute strength. For all Reynard's trickery, the foxes that appear in East Asian mythology are more powerful.

The *huli jing* ('fox spirit') was first mentioned in ancient Chinese literature in 333 BC. It is a red fox that can grow up to nine tails, adding a new one every century, and increasing its powers, even becoming immortal. The *huli jing* can give omens, and seeing one can also be a positive sign. Yu the Great, the semi-mythical founder of China's first ruling dynasty, the Xia, who rose to become king through popular acclaim after controlling the flooding waters of the Yellow River, saw a nine-tailed fox before he accomplished any of his great deeds. As the *huli jing* ages, it gains the ability to shape-shift into human form, often posing as a beautiful woman. It interacts with people for both good and ill; on one hand it can cure illnesses, but on the other it can possess them and wreak havoc. One was said to have possessed Daji (*c.* 1076–1046 BC), favourite consort of Di Xin (d. 1046 BC), final king of the Shang dynasty, which ruled China from *c.* 1600–1046 BC. Daji became a malign influence at court, prompting Di Xin to depravity. To amuse Daji he harshly tortured his enemies and levied high taxes to fund their debauchery (including building a wine-filled pool overhung by skewers of roasted meat). Di Xin's rule ended when he was overthrown by Wu, ruler of a state from the west, who had Daji put to death. Wu then established the Zhou dynasty, which reigned until 256 BC. Such stories, which stress the evil of the later Shang, are products of Zhou-era historians and writers, and were largely promulgated to help justify their seizure of the throne.

These Chinese legends spread to Japan, where they inspired the *kitsune*, as well as a similar figure in Korea called the *kumiho*. Like the *huli jing*, *kitsune* are foxes with up to nine tails who are capable of both good and evil. Some, called *zenko*, are benevolent and wise figures who often appear as priests and help solve disputes. They serve Inari, the deity of well-being, rice and prosperity (similarly, in Mesopotamian mythology, foxes are the messengers of Ninhursag, a fertility goddess). In comparison, *yako* are evil and destructive, using their powers to steal things and ruin reputations. *Kitsune* have various powers, which increase as they age, including the ability to fly, breathe fire, control the weather and see the future. They are most known for being able to turn into humans. Their disguise is never perfect though. Sometimes they are given away by their tail or ears remaining visible, while their shadows or reflections may show their true form. They also always carry a glowing ball called a *hoshi-no-tama*, which helps give them their magical powers. *Kitsune* also have trouble saying some words, notably *moshi*, which is why Japanese people often answer the telephone by saying *moshi-moshi* – it shows the caller there is not a potentially malevolent fox spirit on the line.

The mythology of the red fox echoes their real-life swiftness, versatility and ability to overcome obstacles. Traditionally, they have lived in rural areas, where their diet mainly consists of a wide range of small mammals (meaning they play a key role in controlling rodent numbers), as well as eggs, fruit and birds. As they are skilled climbers and persistent burrowers, they can make their way into enclosures of small farm animals, particularly chickens. As foxes will often cache surplus food to eat later, they have been known to kill entire flocks. Since the twentieth century, red foxes also spread to suburban and urban areas. Household refuse and waste has become a key part of their diet; as a result of their strong stomachs and immune systems, they are able to eat virtually anything, even rotten food. Living in these environments may even have changed their physiology; red foxes from towns and cities tend to have shorter, stronger snouts that are better suited to breaking open packaging. Even if it is sometimes viewed as a nuisance, the red fox shows the ability of the animal world to adjust to the growing footprint of mankind on nature.

ANANSI

Another of the most ingenious and quick-witted characters in mythology is Anansi, a shape-shifting spider who originated in West Africa before enslaved people spread his stories to the Caribbean and Americas. He is variously depicted as a trickster, a wise teacher or even playing a role in Creation.

LIONS

The Chauvet Cave, in southern France, contains some of the oldest and best preserved examples of Stone Age art. Painted around 30,000 BC, they mostly depict wild animals, including bears, mammoths and deer. One of the most commonly appearing animals is the lion, showing that humanity's fascination with this species goes back millennia.

Almost all wild lions live in the savannas and grasslands of sub-Saharan Africa, but 12,000 years ago they lived across Africa, Eurasia and the Americas. As human populations grew and their methods of hunting became more sophisticated, they posed an increasing threat to both the lions themselves and their food supply. In addition, the emergence of agriculture led to habitat loss. Therefore, lions had disappeared from the Americas by 10,000 years ago and were largely extinct in Europe by 2,000 years ago. Meanwhile, in Asia the distribution of lions steadily declined. Where once they had lived across the Middle East and into the Indian subcontinent, there are now only around 650 left, all of which live in Gir National Park in Gujarat in western India.

The only social big cats, lions live in prides of around fifteen (although they have been known to reach forty). They usually consist of two to four males, five to ten females and their young. Male lions tend to be about 20 per cent larger, and are distinguished by their manes, whose purpose may be to impress potential mates, intimidate rivals or protect the neck. Lionesses form the core membership of a pride, tending to stay with them for life. Males usually leave their prides at around three, becoming nomadic. After a few years, they may attempt to join another pride. They will often ally with other nomads to enter the tribe by force, killing rival males and cubs. In these cases, lionesses will band together to try to defend their young. Each pride guards its territory, which ranges in size from 20 square kilometres to around 400 (nearly 8 to over 150 square miles), against rivals, patrolling its fringes and demarcating it by scent-marking and roaring at dawn and dusk. Lions feed on animals ranging in size from rodents to giraffes, hunting individually or in coordinated attacks. They stalk their prey and then pounce on it, tearing at the neck. Once the prey has been brought down, the pack rush in and feed. Lions will also eat carrion and scavenge kills of other animals. Such activities are balanced by resting, sleeping and sitting, which lions spend over twenty hours a day doing.

Known as the 'King of the Beasts', lions are a global symbol for dignity, power and courage. They are also linked to royalty and nobility, and often appear on flags and coats of arms. The lion was also the symbol of the Babylonian Empire, one of the dominant forces in the ancient Middle East. Since the late twelfth century AD, it has also featured prominently in the royal arms of England, a tradition established by King Richard I (1157–99), who was popularly known as the 'Lionheart' for his martial valour. England is not alone in using the lion in its national heraldry; it features in the coat of arms of several other countries, including the Czech Republic, Finland and Sri Lanka.

Lions play an important role in the Judaeo-Christian tradition. The lion was the symbol of Judah, son of the Hebrew patriarch Jacob, the grandson of Abraham, founder of Judaism. Judah's tribe eventually became the most powerful and important of the Twelve Tribes of Israel. One of the members of the Tribe of Judah was David, who in around 1000 BC conquered the city of Jerusalem and established the unified Kingdom of Israel. After the death of his son and successor, Solomon, in around 930 BC, Israel was divided, and it was eventually conquered by foreign powers. Before Solomon died, it was said he had a son with the Queen of Sheba, a semi-mythical ruler who had travelled to Jerusalem. According to some traditions, she came from Ethiopia, and the son she had with Solomon was called Menilek. The rulers of the Ethiopian Empire, established in 1270, claimed direct descent from Menilek and used the Lion of Judah as their emblem. The final Emperor of Ethiopia was Haile Selassie I (1892–1975), overthrown by a communist military dictatorship in 1974. He is a central figure in Rastafarianism, a religious movement founded in Jamaica during the 1930s that views him as a messianic figure. For this reason, Rastafarians adopted the Lion of Judah as one of their central symbols. Finally, in the Book of Revelation, a lion symbolizes Christ's second coming.

For all that lions have been respected, humans have also exploited and mistreated them, few more so than the ancient Romans. A central part of ancient Roman life was its games, spectacular events put on by elites to curry popular favour. They originated as a funerary rite in 242 BC, when two sons marked their father's death by having slaves fight each other. This developed into displays of public combat, often, but not always, to the death, between trained 'gladiators' (named after the short swords many of them used). When the first gladiators

THE TSAVO MAN-EATERS

Lions usually avoid people and generally fear them, but attacks on humans are not uncommon. Sometimes individual lions or prides will develop a habit of feeding on humans. This occurred in 1898 in Tsavo in Kenya, when a pair of lions targeted the campsites of workers building a railway bridge, killing over thirty people. This brought construction to a halt; it only restarted when the two lions were killed.

and wild animals games was held in 189 BC, lions were selected as their foe. Over time, the games developed into a highly elaborate and costly spectacle. This culminated in AD 80 in the construction of the Colosseum in Rome, a vast amphitheatre that seated over 50,000 spectators. Underneath it was a series of tunnels and chambers that housed an elaborate system of cogs, pulleys and weights that allowed cages filled with wild animals to be lifted to the arena floor. Most games started with the *venatio*, where wild beasts, including ostriches, rhinos and bears, fought each other and hunters. Next followed the *damnatio ad bestias*, where criminals (including early Christians, who were subject to state persecution) were put to death by being made to fight wild animals, usually unarmed. Sometimes the condemned were lashed to stakes. The animals involved, including lions, were often mistreated and starved so they would be more ferocious and bloodthirsty. The 'entertainment' ended with the main event: combat between gladiators. In AD 380, Christianity became the state religion of the Roman Empire. This hastened the decline of gladiatorial combat, the subject of criticism by Christians, although public displays of fights with and between wild animals remained popular until the late seventh century.

There are now no more than 25,000 lions still living in the wild. They face the problem of human encroachment, in the form of farms and ranches, on their lands, as well as poaching and diseases spread to them by other species. However, it is hoped that conservation efforts and the creation of protected areas will ensure their long-term survival.

SNAKES

The snake occupies a dual position in mythology: it can be a symbol of evil and deception but also stand for creation and healing. Regardless of how they have been viewed, it is undeniable that snakes have long been the subject of fascination.

Snakes are found in every corner of the Earth with the exception of Antarctica, Greenland, Iceland, Ireland, Hawaii and New Zealand. There are over 3,400 species, including around sixty that live in the sea. All are predators and swallow their prey whole, with some having the capability to stretch their jaws wide enough to consume animals three times larger than their head. These include the boas, which kill prey by coiling their bodies around them and squeezing them to death. To help them hunt, snakes have forked tongues to smell their surroundings, and openings called 'pit holes' in front of their eyes that sense body heat. They also have bones in their lower jaw that pick up the vibrations from the movement of animals. The rattlesnake has hardened layers of epidermis at the end of its tail, which it rapidly shakes to produce a distinctive noise that warns off other animals.

About one-fifth of snakes produce venom, which can paralyse prey or potential threats. The most toxic belongs to the inland taipan of Australia, whose venom causes paralysis, muscle damage and haemorrhaging. Some species, notably many cobras, spit venom, aiming to blind the target. It has been argued that humans have an innate fear of snakes and arachnids, which is an evolutionary mechanism that goes back to the danger of their bites. Only around 200 snakes can kill or seriously wound humans and, as they are shy and solitary animals, they will only strike when bothered. Snakes have other qualities that have made them the subject of reverence and awe. To make room for growth and combat parasites, snakes frequently shed their skin, meaning they can often symbolize immortality and rebirth. In addition, snakes have lidless eyes covered by a transparent epidermis; this produces an unblinking stare that invokes wisdom and omniscience.

Snakes are particularly reviled in the Judaeo-Christian tradition. This has its origins in the Book of Genesis, and the talking serpent that tempted Eve into eating the forbidden fruit from the tree of the knowledge of good and evil. This disobedience led to the 'fall of man', and the ejection of Adam and Eve from the Garden of Eden. For its role in the episode, the serpent was cursed by God to crawl on the ground and be the subject of mankind's revulsion. This enmity is not shared by many other religions and cultures, which generally regard snakes more positively, even placing them at the centre of their creation stories.

A popular feature of Mesoamerican religion is the 'Feathered Serpent' god. In Aztec mythology, he was known as Quetzalcoatl, god of wind and learning, and a force of harmony and balance. He played a central role in creation. Just before our present world (the Aztecs believed it was the fifth to exist) was created, there was a giant flood. The waters were home to a terrifying sea monster called Tlaltecuhtli. Quetzalcoatl worked with his brother, and sometime rival, Tezcatlipoca to defeat him. They both turned into serpents and killed Tlaltecuhtli, tearing his body in two. One half became the sky and stars, and the other the Earth. Quetzalcoatl then journeyed to the underworld to collect the bones of people who had lived in previous worlds, creating the present version of humanity. He then located a 'food mountain' full of maize, seeds and grain that he arranged for another god to split open, meaning people would have something to eat. Finally, Quetzalcoatl helped to create the maguey plant, which could be used to make the alcoholic drink pulque, which brought humanity joy. The snake also appears in Chinese creation myths, where the origin of mankind goes back to Fuxi and Nüwa, a brother and sister who had human heads but the body of a snake. They used clay to create the first humans; together they taught them to cook, hunt, fish and write.

In spite of their sometimes venomous nature, snakes are often imbued with restorative, protective powers. The

Rod of Asclepius, a serpent entwined around a staff that belonged to the ancient Greek god of healing, has become a global symbol for medicine and physicians. Other traditions go beyond imagery to make more direct use of snakes. The Hopi, a Native American tribe indigenous to the Southwestern United States, make use of snakes in one of their most important and long-standing rituals. In late August, they perform the 'snake dance', a ceremony that gives thanks to the spirits and helps bring fertility and good fortune to the Earth. Snakes are gathered from four directions and placed in a *kiva*, an underground room, where they are purified by being bathed in yucca-root suds and then placed in a structure made of branches. After at least nine days, the only part of the ceremony that can be viewed by the public takes place: participants emerge from the *kiva* dancing with the snakes, holding them in their mouths and wrapping them around their necks and bodies. The snakes are then released to carry the message that the Hopi are living harmoniously with nature. Elsewhere in the United States there is another, more recent custom of using snakes in religious worship. 'Snake handling' began in a handful of Protestant churches in rural Appalachia, where pastors and congregants handle and pass around venomous snakes (as well as sometimes drinking poison). This is based on a literal reading of the New Testament where Jesus tells his disciples he has given them the ability to pick up or trample on snakes without harm coming to them. Those who take part in the practice are well aware of the lethal risks, but they believe their actions show their obedience to God and faith in Him. Despite being made illegal in some states and several deaths, the practice still continues in over a hundred churches. It shows just how powerful the draw of snakes can be.

DOVES

Doves, especially those that are white-feathered, have been a symbol of gentleness, peace, love and divinity for millennia. Along with pigeons, generally a far less venerated bird, they are members of the *Columbidae* family, which contains 344 species. The precise distinction between doves and pigeons is hazy. Although in the anglophone world the smaller members of the *Columbidae* family were generally referred to as doves, there is a great deal of variation and inconsistency in how the terms are used. Indeed, they can be somewhat interchangeable depending on context. The common pigeon, for example, is merely a feral version of domesticated rock doves.

The link between doves and love goes back to the ancient world, and may have originated because they were believed to mate for life (observation of them in the wild shows that they may indeed retain breeding partners far longer than other birds). They were one of the symbols of the Sumerian goddess Inanna, the Queen of Heaven and patron of love, fertility, sex and war, who was later venerated across Mesopotamia as Ishtar. Dove figurines have been found at temples devoted to her dating back as far as 4500 BC. Doves were also linked to the ancient Greek goddess of love Aphrodite, as well as her Roman equivalent, Venus, whose chariot they were said to pull.

A particularly strong symbol of affection and companionship is the turtle dove. Their name has nothing to do with reptiles but derives from what they are known as in Latin: *turtur*, which onomatopoeically refers to their distinctive 'turr-turr' song. William Shakespeare (1564–1616) mentions them in his plays and poems several times as symbols of devotion (often just calling them 'turtles'). The European turtle dove is migratory and spends the winter in sub-Saharan Africa, meaning that its return to Europe heralds the coming of spring and flowers coming into bloom. In addition, thanks to their mention in 'The Twelve Days of Christmas', a pair of turtle doves is a common festive decoration.

Doves play a central role in Christian symbolism. This goes back to the Book of Genesis, and the Great Flood God sent to cleanse the world of sin. The only righteous man, Noah, was forewarned, and built an ark for himself, along with seven pairs of every 'clean' animal and one pair of every 'unclean' one. The rains fell for forty days and forty nights, flooding the Earth, but Noah's ark safely floated on the waters. After 150 days, the floodwater began to recede. Noah then sent out a raven to search for dry land, before releasing a dove. Initially, the dove found nowhere to land and returned to the ark. Noah waited a week then released it again; this time it returned with an olive leaf, proving the flood had receded. God had made peace with mankind; the world was now ready for Noah and his family, as well as the animals he had saved, to return. The dove also represents the Holy Spirit, the third part of the Holy Trinity. When John the Baptist baptized Jesus Christ in the River Jordan, the Gospel of Matthew records that the Holy Spirit descended on him in the form of a dove, showing he was the Son of God. The dove and olive branch thus often appeared on the tombs of members of the early Church, and is a common and lasting feature in Christian artwork.

Pelicans

Aside from doves, another bird that frequently appears in Christian imagery is the pelican. This is because of the myth that, if food was scarce, the mother pelican would feed her young with her own blood by pecking her breast. This self-sacrifice linked the pelican to Jesus dying for the sins of mankind.

Extending from what they represent in Christianity – the tranquillity of the soul through baptism – doves have become a near universal symbol of pacifism and peace between nations. In this spirit, when the Olympics were revived in Athens in 1896, white 'doves of peace' were ceremonially released (this also referenced the homing pigeons sent out to spread news of victors at the ancient games). This continued until the Seoul Olympics of 1988, when several unfortunate doves were incinerated when they perched on the cauldron just before it was lit. Doves were released at the 1992 Barcelona Olympics well in advance of the ignition of the ceremonial cauldron, but since then no live birds have been involved.

The release of doves has thus become a common occurrence at meetings and political rallies; none more famously than when the Cuban socialist leader Fidel Castro (1926–2016) made a speech in Havana on 8 January 1959. Castro was a former lawyer who had opposed the American-backed military junta led by Colonel Fulgencio Batista (1901–73). His insurrectionary actions had led to imprisonment and then exile to Mexico in 1955, but he returned the next year at the head of a revolutionary group that fought a guerrilla campaign that led to the collapse of Batista's regime on New Year's Day 1959. Therefore, when Castro addressed the people of Havana one week later, it was part victory speech, part assurance of a stable and peaceful future. Castro, still wearing his army fatigues, requested all Cubans unite behind his vision of revolutionary, yet peaceful, reform of the country. As his speech was coming to an end, white doves were released. One landed on his shoulder and two more on his lectern; they continued to perch there while he concluded his remarks, where he pledged not to use force and to rule only at the pleasure of the people. The apparent comfort and ease with which the doves remained on Castro was a powerful image and did much to consolidate popular support behind him. Later on, his enemies would accuse Castro of faking the event and somehow training or coercing the doves using magnets, but no definitive proof emerged to confirm these suspicions. Castro successfully established a one-party communist state that, despite near-constant opposition from the USA, has remained in place since then, continuing even after he stepped down as leader in 2011.

Bats

. . . .

There are over 1,200 species of bat, the only mammal capable of flight. For the most part, they are nocturnal animals, roosting, sometimes in colonies numbering in the millions, by day and seeking food at night. They navigate by echolocation, emitting short, high-frequency pulses of sound and then determining the location of objects and features of the landscape by listening to their echoes. Their hearing is excellent, aided by their extremely large, and sometimes funnel-shaped, ears. Bats are by no means blind; many species have sight even stronger than humans.

Much of the mythology surrounding bats is associated with the fact that they have attributes characteristic of both birds and mammals. In one of the fables of the ancient Greek storyteller Aesop (*c.* 620–564 BC), the bat escapes the clutches of a bird- and mouse-eating weasel by claiming to be neither (in fact the bat is more closely related to primates than rodents). In another fable there was a conflict between birds and land animals, and the bat joined whichever side was in the ascendant. This meant that when peace came, the bat was rejected by both sides, and so was condemned to only come out at night. Similarly, in the mythologies of Native American peoples the origin of the bat is associated with a competitive ball game between birds and land animals. The bat, then a wingless small creature, wanted to join the land animals but was rejected – the eagle then gave him wings so he could join the birds (in another telling the inverse is the case, and the bat is given teeth by land animals when turned away from the birds).

As bats are nocturnal they often symbolize death and darkness. Their dual nature as both winged and mammalian has led many to link them to the uncanny and mysterious, often with a link to the underworld (for example, in Tongan mythology they are associated with the souls of the dead). As such, bats are often tied to Halloween, as well as the Celtic festival Samhain that occurs at the same time of the year and marks the end of the harvest. Most famously, bats have become a central part of the lore of vampires – supernatural undead creatures that feed on blood. This is a relatively recent connection. Although in some European traditions they were believed to be messengers for the Devil and used by witches as their familiars, it was not until the eighteenth and nineteenth centuries that the connection between bats and vampires became commonplace. This was largely thanks to the work of the Irish author Bram Stoker (1847–1912), in whose famed Gothic horror *Dracula* (1897) the eponymous main character has the ability to shape-shift into a bat.

The link between feasting on blood and bats is not wholly fallacious. There was some element of truth to it: three species of bat are indeed sanguivorous (blood-sucking). Vampire bats, named after the figure in folklore, are all native to Latin America. They feed on sleeping mammals, biting them using their sharp incisor teeth; their saliva includes a strong anticoagulant that stops the blood from clotting, allowing them to lap it up. As the vampire bat's bite is shallow, its prey remains asleep throughout the feeding, which takes up to thirty minutes. They seldom feed on humans but their bites provide egg-laying sites for parasites and they sometimes spread diseases like rabies.

In Mesoamerica, the region extending from central Mexico to northern Costa Rica, bats are frequently tied to death, sacrifice and destruction. This may reflect the direct experience of these peoples living with vampire bats and incidents of them feeding on humans. In Mesoamerican art, bats are often depicted with human bones and sometimes have snouts shaped like sacrificial knives. In the mythology of the Maya, an ancient Mesoamerican civilization that emerged in modern-day Guatemala, northern Belize and southern Mexico, one of their gods is called Camazotz ('death bat') who is a cave-dwelling creature that drinks human blood. Camazotz is also the name of monstrous bats that feature in the *Popul Vuh*, a collection of epic myths of the Quiché, who are one of the Maya peoples. Two of the main characters are Hunahpu and Xbalanque, the 'Hero Twins' who travel to Xibalba (the Maya underworld) to fight its gods. On their journey they are subjected to a number of trials, including spending a night in the House of Bats. To escape being attacked by Camazotz, the twins shrink themselves into their blowguns but disaster strikes when Hunahpu sticks his head out and is decapitated. Fortunately, his brother Xbalanque fashions a new head out of a squash and together they ultimately defeat the lords of the underworld. Eventually, Hunahpu and Xbalanque become the moon and sun, respectively, and their story represents the triumph of light over dark. Even so, Camazotz remained feared, and the Maya would plant their corn at the time of year when he descended into Xibalba, so he would not interfere.

Bats are not always viewed negatively. The ancient Egyptians believed they would ward away ailments such as poor eyesight, toothache, fever and even baldness, and in Poland they are a symbol of luck. But it is in China that bats have the most positive associations; they are linked to happiness and good fortune, while five of them together symbolizes the *wufu*, the 'five blessings' of virtue, long life, wealth, health and a natural death. This favourable view of bats echoes the many benefits they have for humans. As the vast majority of bats are insect eaters, they play a vital role in controlling their numbers, particularly for species like the mosquito. In addition, the bats who eat pollen and nectar are essential to the propagation of numerous species of plant, including the banana and the agave (the source of tequila). Finally, bat guano is an excellent fertilizer. The bat, therefore, deserves to be seen not as a frightening symbol of darkness but as a resourceful and incredible animal.

JAGUARS

Largest of the extant New World big cats, jaguars live in remote areas of Central and South America, although their range once extended from Patagonia to the Southwestern United States. Apex predators whose diet consists of at least eighty-five other species (including armadillos, crocodiles, fish and birds), jaguars are solitary creatures and mainly hunt at night, stalking and ambushing their prey, usually by leaping on it from above. Unlike other big cats, which target the throat or underbelly, jaguars bite into the skull of their quarry, aiming to kill it by penetrating into the brain. Their bite is so powerful it can pierce even the shell of a turtle. Jaguars are also able swimmers, and have even been observed swimming across the Panama Canal. Jaguars are currently threatened by poachers, who target them for their distinctive spotted coats. An even more serious threat to the survival of the 15,000 remaining jaguars is loss of habitat due to deforestation for logging and farming. Once, though, they were worshipped and revered as representations of strength and power in numerous pre-Columbian American cultures, particularly in Mesoamerica.

The first major Mesoamerican civilization were the Olmecs, who had emerged in modern-day southern Mexico by 1200 BC. They built several cities, and developed a writing system and a sophisticated calendar. They also may have popularized the Mesoamerican ball game, a sport played on a court where the players aimed to bounce a solid rubber ball through a stone hoop. The game had a ritual aspect, as the ball symbolized the sun moving through the sky. When played as part of ceremonial events, participants wore elaborate costumes, including helmets that resembled jaguar heads. The Olmecs held jaguars in high esteem, believing they were able to cross into the spirit world. This was because jaguars hunt both by day and by night and on land and in water. Olmec rulers sought to justify their status through emphasizing their connection to the jaguar, claiming they descended directly from a union between the animal and a human. Sculptures and carvings of figures with a mixture of jaguar and human features were common in Olmec art. Known as 'were-jaguars', they had round, infant-like faces, downturned mouths, fleshy lips, canine teeth and almond-shaped eyes. The Olmec civilization went into decline after 400 BC, possibly due to environmental changes that decreased agricultural productivity.

Olmec culture and religion was highly influential on other Mesoamerican cultures. They included the Maya, which arose in modern-day southern Mexico, Guatemala and northern Belize. Between the third and tenth centuries AD, there were over forty Maya cities, which featured great plazas, pyramids, palaces and temples. Ruling these cities were rival kings, who claimed semi-divine status. To display their power and right to rule, they frequently wore jaguar pelts and necklaces made of their teeth, and their thrones featured carvings of the animal. The Maya practised human sacrifice to please and appease their many gods (several of whom were in the form of jaguars). They also sacrificed jaguars, and it is possible there was a long-distance trade in the animals to supply Maya kings with them. After *c.* AD 900, Maya cities were largely abandoned. The reason for this is uncertain, although warfare, overpopulation and overuse of land have all been posited. The Maya people largely retreated to living in villages, and their great cities were gradually reclaimed by the rainforest.

The final indigenous civilization to flourish in Mesoamerica was the Aztec Empire. It was founded by a people called the Mexica, who migrated into central Mexico from the north in around 1250. During the mid-fourteenth century, they founded a settlement called Tenochtitlan on a swampy island in the middle of Lake Texcoco. Over the next 150 years, it grew into a major city with a population of over 200,000; it was filled with dozens of monumental buildings, laid out on a grid and connected to the mainland by three great causeways. Meanwhile, the Aztec kings established a triple alliance with two nearby city states. With the Aztecs as the leading partner, they together embarked on a series of conquests that saw them become the dominant force in the region. Jaguars were as important to the Aztecs as to earlier Mesoamerican cultures. One of their main gods, Tezcatlipoca, was synonymous with the jaguar, often appearing in its form. The Aztecs built up a strong army, and soldiers who fought bravely and captured enemies were granted high status, and allowed to become jaguar warriors. This was a military order whose members were full-time soldiers. They wore uniforms that evoked the jaguar, hoping to be imbued with its fighting spirit (there was also a similar order called the eagle warriors).

The power and glory of the Aztec Empire would be brought down at the hands of the Spanish conquistador

Hernán Cortés (1485–1547), who arrived in Mexico in 1519. He and his men were allowed to enter Tenochtitlan and given a guardedly hospitable welcome. Tensions arose with the Aztec inhabitants and the Spanish were forced out the following year. Cortés was not to be deterred; he returned to besiege the city in May 1521, along with his local allies. By this time, Western diseases, to which the indigenous population had no immunity, were reaching epidemic proportions. This, combined with Spanish cavalry, firearms and steel weapons and armour, helped lead Cortés to victory. Tenochtitlan fell on 13 August, signalling the end of the Aztec Empire and heralding the beginning of Spanish colonial dominance of its former realms, which eventually extended across all of Mesoamerica.

4

Science, Health
and Medicine

·· ❧ ❧ ··

Fleas

. . . .

Despite measuring only around 2.5 millimetres (around 0.1 inches), fleas have caused three of the most serious pandemics in human history. Fleas are wingless parasitic insects that feed on the blood of mammals and birds, causing inflammation and itching. As they lack wings, they have developed powerful legs that allow them to jump over 200 times their body length, meaning they can travel from host to host, while backward-projecting spines on the legs anchor them to hair, fur and feathers. There are over 3,000 species and subspecies of flea, but only about a dozen will commonly feed on humans. In doing so, they act as vectors for infection and disease. Cat fleas, for example, can spread tapeworms and a form of typhus to humans. The deadliest is the Oriental rat flea, which usually infests rodents but will readily spread to any mammal, and is infamous for carrying a bacteria called *Yersinia pestis*, which causes plague.

Yersinia pestis forms colonies in the valve that connects the flea's throat to its gut, making it harder for them to swallow blood. This does not kill them but makes them hungrier and encourages them to feed more As they try to suck up the blood, it dislodges some of the bacteria, which is then ejected into the animal it is feeding on, infecting them. Between one day and a week after exposure to *Yersinia pestis*, symptoms of plague appear: headaches, nausea, fever and diarrhoea. This can develop into the three forms of plague. The main one is bubonic plague, named after buboes, which are painful, swollen lymph nodes around the armpit, groin and neck – this causes death in 40 to 60 per cent of cases. If the infection moves to the lungs, it causes a secondary form – pneumonic plague. If it moves to the bloodstream, it leads to septicemic plague. The latter two types of plague can be spread by contact with infected droplets in breath, sputum and blood, and, if left untreated, are usually fatal.

By the late fifth century, the Western Roman Empire had fragmented under foreign invasions, while in the East it continued as the Byzantine Empire. The Byzantine emperors saw themselves as the direct heirs to Rome's imperial mantle. The one who came closest to restoring the Roman Empire was Justinian I (AD 485–565), who ascended the throne in 527. Under his rule North Africa was recovered from the Vandals, Italy and Dalmatia from the Ostrogoths, and southern Spain from the Visigoths. Plague undermined Justinian's achievements. In 541, there was an outbreak in Egypt and by the next year it had spread to Constantinople in grain ships, before being carried throughout the Mediterranean on shipping routes. This initial outbreak killed 25 million, and a similar number died before the pandemic ended around 750. The outbreak seriously weakened Byzantine strength, and within a century of Justinian's death most of his conquests had been lost.

The second plague pandemic was far more serious. It began in Central or East Asia during the 1330s, and was carried into the Middle East along overland trade routes. By 1347, it had already killed millions. That year, fleas, rats and people infected with *Yersinia pestis* arrived in Sicily, carried by trade ships from Crimea. Over the next five years, it spread across Europe and North Africa. In total, this 'Black Death' killed at least 75 million, and in some areas, particularly heavily urbanized ones, mortality rates exceeded 80 per cent. Contemporaries were unaware of the flea's role in spreading the plague. Instead, some blamed 'bad air' carrying poisonous vapours and tried to combat infection by burning incense, flowers and wood. People also took purgatives and subjected themselves to bloodletting, neither of which helped. In the Christian world, the plague was seen as divine punishment for sin. In response, groups of 'flagellants' began publicly scourging themselves, hoping to assuage God's anger; others looked for a scapegoat, violently targeting outsider groups. The Jewish population was the focus of anti-Semitic attacks, which were often tacitly approved or encouraged by local rulers. The only truly effective way of fighting the disease was the quarantine – named after the forty-day period the Venetians would isolate visiting ships for.

Although the Black Death ended in 1353, plague remained endemic in many areas and periodic local outbreaks (such as occurred in London in 1665–6 and Marseilles in 1720) killed thousands. There were some benefits for survivors, who could demand higher wages and better working conditions as a result of shortage of labour. In Western Europe, the Black Death helped end feudalism, meaning peasants were no longer bound to a piece of land with an obligation to perform labour or pay dues to their lord. In Eastern Europe, which was generally more sparsely populated and less affected by plague, the nobility consolidated their control of the peasantry, which meant serfdom continued there into the eighteenth and nineteenth centuries.

The third and final plague pandemic originated in Southwest China during the mid-nineteenth century. By then, globalization had gathered pace, creating transcontinental shipping routes that spread *Yersinia pestis*-carrying fleas to port cities across the world. Plague had spread to every inhabited continent by

1910, although it was most serious in China and India. Fortunately, by this point scientific and medical advances meant there was a better understanding of the spread of diseases, as well as how to treat them. By the 1890s, there was a general acceptance of 'germ theory', and it was understood diseases were spread by tiny particles called pathogens. In 1894, the Swiss-French physician Alexandre Yersin (1863–1943) identified the bacteria responsible for plague, which was named after him. Four years later, the French biologist Paul-Louis Simond (1858–1947) determined it was fleas who spread the plague. This allowed governments to better control outbreaks and led to the creation of plague vaccines. By the 1920s, major outbreaks had ceased but the pandemic was not declared over until 1960. There are still occasional local outbreaks of plague, although it can now be treated with antibiotics, meaning that the flea should never again pose such a serious threat to public health.

LEECHES

. . . .

Ancient Greek physicians believed in 'humours' – four bodily fluids (blood, phlegm, yellow bile and black bile) that governed a person's health and personality. It was imperative to keep a balance between them, as if there was a surfeit or lack of a humour it could lead to illness. These ideas were embraced by Galen (AD 129–201), a Greek physician and surgeon from Anatolia, then part of the Roman Empire. Many of his writings were translated into Arabic, popularizing his theories in the Islamic world. In the eleventh century, Galen's extensive corpus was translated into Latin and reintroduced to Western Europe. They remained standard medical texts until the mid-sixteenth century. According to the theory of humours, excess blood was a major health problem, causing a range of problems including headaches, fever and strokes. It could be addressed through 'purging', where patients were given substances that induced vomiting, urination or diarrhoea, or 'bloodletting'. A popular method of drawing blood was applying leeches to the skin.

Leeches are segmented worms that mostly live in freshwater. Around three-quarters of the over 650 species of leech are parasitic and feed by sucking blood from other animals, while the rest are predators who eat small invertebrates. Parasitic leeches generally have three sets of jaws filled with dozens of sharp teeth that they use to bite their hosts. To keep their grip while they feed they also have a sucker at their posterior that attaches to the host's body. Their saliva contains substances that anaesthetize the area around the incision, dilate blood vessels to increase blood flow, and prevent clotting. When the leech has fed enough (sometimes consuming ten times its body weight), it will detach and not have to feed again for up to a year. Often the host will not even realize they have been fed on. The smallest leeches are around 5 millimetres (0.2 inches) long, while the largest is the giant Amazon leech, which grows to 45 centimetres (nearly 18 inches) long and 10 centimetres (4 inches) wide. The European medicinal leech, the one most commonly used in bloodletting, is about 20 centimetres (8 inches) long.

The leech has been used in medicine since ancient times; the Egyptians believed it could treat flatulence, while the Roman author and naturalist Pliny the Elder (AD 23/4–79) prescribed their use to combat phlebitis and haemorrhoids. Medieval physicians, encouraged by the widespread belief in humours, used leeches to treat numerous issues including urinary problems, inflammation and eye diseases. Even after the system of humours was challenged in the mid-sixteenth century and proved to be inaccurate, doctors still often prescribed bloodletting, meaning leeches continued to be a common treatment. Their use peaked in the mid-nineteenth century, largely thanks to the Frenchman François-Joseph-Victor Broussais (1772–1838), a former military surgeon.

He believed all maladies started as a result of irritation in the gastrointestinal tract and from there spread to other parts of the body. According to Broussais, one of the best ways to restore health was mild bloodletting. As such, he preferred leeches to making incisions, because they were gentler – he was once said to have attached ninety to a single patient. Broussais's ideas became incredibly popular, and led to a huge surge in demand for leeches.

Traditionally, leeches were gathered by 'gardeners', who waded into ponds with their legs exposed. They then stored the leeches that had attached themselves in rainwater-filled jars and sold them. These methods were not enough to satisfy the emerging 'leech craze'. Instead, elderly horses would be cut in several places and then driven into leech ponds. Later, 'leecheries' were created by digging ponds and stocking them with leeches. As a result of unnatural conditions and overcrowding, these farmed leeches often suffered from diseases. Indeed, many patients and doctors would demand wild leeches, believing them to be superior. There was high demand for leeches in the United States; although there were many local species there, imported European ones were preferred. The demand grew so great that it drove the European medicinal leech to the point of extinction, and they now only exist in small, scattered populations. By the second half of the nineteenth century, as diseases began to be better understood, doctors were questioning the benefits of bloodletting, and its practice declined.

Since the 1970s, there has been a resurgence in the medical use of leeches, known as hirudotherapy. They are particularly useful after reconstructive or plastic surgery. When applied, the substances in their saliva improve blood flow in areas with poor circulation (for example, if a digit has been reattached or a skin graft), allowing small veins to knit together and heal. The natural anticoagulant they release also improves the blood flow, and helps prevent inflammation and the tissue from drying out. The benefits of their application continue for ten hours after the leech has finished feeding. Whereas the same leech was once used for multiple patients, now, to prevent infection, they are humanely destroyed after being used on one. It is also possible that the application of leeches may help to relieve inflammation, pain and stiffness caused by arthritis. Leeches are now 'farmed' in laboratories and transported in refrigerated containers. Although their use pales in comparison to their nineteenth-century heyday, leeches continue to play a role in healing.

DODOS

. . . .

Lying over 1,900 kilometres (1,180 miles) off the coast of mainland Africa in the Indian Ocean, Mauritius is a tropical island surrounded by a coral reef. It was created over 8 million years ago as a result of underwater volcanic activity. Due to its isolation, it developed unique flora and fauna that existed in the rainforest that covered most of the island. The first humans to visit the island were Arab and Malay navigators in the tenth century AD, followed by the Portuguese in 1507. The Dutch followed in 1598, naming the island Mauritius after their national leader, Maurice of Nassau (1567–1625). Forty years later, they established a colony there, establishing the first permanent human settlement in Mauritius. This would have a disastrous impact on the island's wildlife, none more so than a flightless bird called the dodo.

The dodo's distant ancestors settled Mauritius by flying there. As genetic evidence suggests its closest living relative is the Nicobar pigeon, a bird that lives in South East Asia and islands in the western Pacific, it is likely the dodo originated from this region. As the dodo had no natural predators on Mauritius, it was able to grow larger, to a height of about 1 metre (over 3 feet), and its ability to fly became unnecessary. As no animals on the island ate their eggs, dodos simply laid them on the ground. Recent studies of dodo remains suggest the bird was capable of moving quite quickly along the ground. It is likely that it stretched out its wings to help it maintain balance (as well as using them in mating displays). Scans of dodo skulls also suggest they had enlarged olfactory bulbs, allowing them to sniff out the fruits that probably formed the majority of their diet. The dodo thus became superbly adapted for conditions on Mauritius, persisting through the volcanic activity, climate shifts, droughts and wildfires that impacted on the island over the millennia. They would not be able to survive contact with humans.

For the Dutch settlers and sailors who arrived on Mauritius, the dodo was a curiosity. Drawings and engravings were made of it, and some specimens were probably sent back to Europe. The dodo was a valuable source of fresh meat – something much desired after long ocean voyages. Although the dodo was certainly hunted for food (and would have been an easy target because it did not fear humans), this was not the main reason for its numbers declining. Archaeological evidence from early Dutch settlements in Mauritius suggests they mainly ate livestock they bought. Rather, the main factor was the Dutch introducing novel species like cats, dogs, goats, deer, monkeys, rats and pigs. These competed with the dodo for food, as well as eating its eggs and chicks. Furthermore, logging robbed the dodo of its habitat. The last living dodo was seen in 1662, and it was extinct by the later seventeenth century. Other species would follow, such as the domed Mauritius giant tortoise, which had disappeared by the early eighteenth century. Even after being wiped out, the dodo would suffer a final indignity: being portrayed as a chubby, ungainly and somewhat comic creature that became a byword for obsolescence.

The earliest drawings of dodos are sketches drawn by eyewitnesses, and show a far slimmer bird than later depictions. During the seventeenth and eighteenth centuries, images of the bird became more fantastical and elaborate, with inaccurate features like excessively large heads and beaks, webbed feet and colourful plumage added (the dodo's feathers were mostly brownish-grey). As some paintings may have been made based on captured specimens that had grown overweight in captivity, the dodo was portrayed as being somewhat fat. This meant that estimates of the dodo's size were exaggerated. Scanning and three-dimensional modelling of dodos suggest a slimmer animal that probably only weighed 10 kilograms (22 pounds), half of what had previously been claimed.

Uncertainty also surrounds the dodo because very few remains of it were preserved effectively. There are no complete specimens and surviving skeletons of it have been assembled from several different dodos. The only surviving soft tissue of the dodo belongs to a mummified specimen now held at the Oxford University Museum of Natural History. This is said to have been a dodo that was brought to London during the 1630s to be displayed to the public (recent scanning of the head found lead pellets embedded in it, opening up the possibility it was shot before leaving Mauritius). After it died, it was stuffed and in 1662 it was given to the antiquary Elias Ashmole (1617–92), who presented it to Oxford. By 1775, due to the less effective taxidermy of the time, the dodo was rotting and only its head and one foot could be salvaged. These body parts thus provide the only known source of dodo DNA, which has allowed the bird to be further studied. In 2016, its genome was sequenced, creating the theoretical possibility that the dodo could be brought back from extinction.

MOA

New Zealand's indigenous people, the Māori, had arrived there from eastern Polynesia by the fourteenth century. Due to its isolation, New Zealand had developed an ecosystem with no native land mammals except bats and unique species of birds, reptiles and frogs. Most impressive were the moa, flightless birds related to the ostrich. They included the giant moa, which stood at over 3 metres (10 feet) high, making it the tallest ever bird. Despite being swift runners, the moa were hunted to extinction by the late seventeenth century, although some smaller species may have lasted until the nineteenth century.

Mosquitoes

. . . .

Apart from humans, the animal that has killed the most people throughout history is the mosquito. This small winged insect's impact far exceeds its size, which ranges from 3 to 19 millimetres (0.1 to 0.7 inches). Mosquitoes flourish in warmer and more humid regions, particularly the tropics, although they can also live in subtropical and temperate conditions. They require some source of water to lay their eggs in, which hatch into aquatic larvae. Consequently, mosquito populations tend to be higher in coastal, swampy and marshy areas. Mosquitoes, though, will lay their eggs in any area of stagnant or standing water, meaning settlements with poor drainage or higher pollution are at greater risk of infestation.

Mosquitoes feed on flower nectar and the juices of fruit. However, these do not contain the iron and protein needed to produce their eggs. To obtain this, female mosquitoes have to suck blood from a host, piercing their skin with their proboscis and injecting an anticoagulant. This prevents the blood clotting and clogging their proboscis while they feed. A mosquito can drink two to three times its bodyweight in blood. In the process, pathogens from the mosquito may infect the host and spread disease.

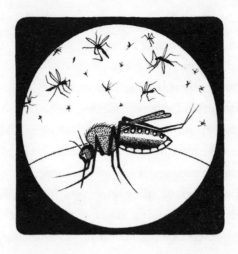

There are 3,500 species of mosquito, which prey on a range of animals including mammals, birds, insects and fish. Over one hundred feed on humans, seeking them out by sensing their temperature, body odour and carbon dioxide emissions. When mosquitoes bite people, they can transmit diseases like dengue fever, encephalitis, filariasis, West Nile fever, yellow fever, Zika fever and, most seriously, malaria, which combine to infect millions of people every year, killing hundreds of thousands. This makes the mosquito one of the greatest threats to public health in the world.

Three groups of mosquito species are most responsible for spreading disease: the *Culex*, *Aedes* and *Anopheles*. *Culex* mosquitoes transmit a range of diseases but most seriously West Nile fever, by spreading the virus that causes it from birds to humans. There is no vaccine for this disease, which 20 per cent of the time causes fever, headaches and vomiting. In about 0.7 per cent of cases, it leads to more serious symptoms and even death.

The *Aedes* mosquitoes originated in Africa. From the fifteenth century AD, European ships, which were primarily carrying enslaved people, unwittingly began to bring them across the Atlantic to the Americas. Since then, they have spread to every continent bar Antarctica; often in used tyres, which, if they contain even some water, can act as a reservoir for their eggs. The *Aedes* spreads a number of diseases, including yellow fever (named after the jaundice it causes in some cases), which can lead to death if untreated. It was once widely believed that poor sanitation or contact with infected people, rather than the mosquito, was the direct cause of yellow fever. This changed thanks to the work of Walter Reed (1851–1902), a US Army surgeon who headed a commission investigating yellow fever after it caused high numbers of deaths during the Spanish–American War of 1898. By 1900, Reed and his team had proved that mosquitoes were responsible, and yellow fever began to be brought under control by reducing mosquito populations through drainage of water and fumigation. During the 1930s, vaccines, which provide lifelong immunity to yellow fever, were developed, but the disease remains endemic in areas of tropical Africa, the Caribbean and Central and South America.

Freshwater Snails

Schistosomiasis is a disease caused by parasitic flatworms released into water by infected freshwater snails. These flatworms contaminate people who come into contact with the infested water, causing infections that can spread to vital organs and cause serious health problems and sometimes death. According to the World Health Organization, it kills around 200,000 people a year, making freshwater snails arguably the second most lethal, non-human animal.

Malaria is the most serious mosquito-borne disease. It is spread only by the *Anopheles*, primarily a species complex called *Anopheles gambiae*. Malaria is a parasitic infection that reproduces in the gut of the mosquito, and is then spread into the bloodstream of humans via the mosquito's saliva. It then enters the liver where it multiplies before re-entering the bloodstream, where it invades and destroys red cells. The malaria virus can then spread into an uninfected mosquito if it bites the host, thus continuing the cycle. Malaria causes chills, fever, aches, nausea, vomiting and diarrhoea. In serious cases, it can disrupt blood flow to vital organs, and, if untreated, lead to comas, seizures and fatality.

The role of the mosquito in spreading malaria was not proved until the later nineteenth century. Before then, it was believed to be caused by 'bad air' (the direct translation of its name) from swamps and marshes. In 1897, Sir Ronald Ross (1857–1932), a British doctor working in India, discovered that the malaria parasite lived in mosquitoes, proving their role in spreading the disease. This was a crucial discovery. Although there are treatments for malaria such as quinine, which comes from the bark of the cinchona tree of the Andes and has been used since the seventeenth century, and anti-malarial drugs like chloroquine developed since 1934, a far more effective way of battling the disease was reducing mosquito populations and preventing them from biting people. This has been done by spraying insecticides, draining swamps and stagnant marshes, as well as more widespread distribution and use of mosquito nets and insect repellents.

Such techniques have led to a decline in malaria, yet in 2018 there were 228 million cases of the disease, leading to 405,000 deaths. The most seriously affected region is sub-Saharan Africa, but it is endemic in areas of Latin America and Asia. Therefore, some researchers propose more drastic solutions, such as genetically engineering mosquitoes so that their offspring die before reaching sexual maturity. In practice, such initiatives would be difficult to enact and they also raise questions about the ethics of potentially wiping out a species.

Guinea Pigs

In around 5000 BC, people in the Andes domesticated a rodent, which they raised for its meat. Aside from the llama and the alpaca, it was the only mammal domesticated for agriculture in the region. By the time of the Incas, who called the creature a *quwi* or *jaca* in their language, Quechua, it was also used in sacrificial ceremonies and its viscera were examined to divine the future. The animal, known in Spanish as the *cuy*, continues to be a food source for many people who live in the Andes. It is known in English as a guinea pig.

In the years after the arrival of the Spanish in the Andes in the 1530s, guinea pigs began making their way back to Europe in small numbers, where they were initially kept as pets by social elites. By the mid-seventeenth century, they had become known as guinea pigs in England, but the precise reason is still unclear. 'Guinea' may refer to the fact that the animals arrived via ports in Guinea in West Africa, or it may be a corrupted form of Guiana, a region in north-eastern South America. They were called pigs because their body shape was seen to be somewhat porcine, and they made squealing noises. By the nineteenth century, guinea pigs, which are generally docile and easy to care for, had become popular pets. These qualities also made them an ideal subject for medical testing.

Humans have been conducting experiments on animals since at least the fourth century BC. As it was taboo, and often illegal, to dissect human cadavers, people wishing to learn more about anatomy often used animals instead. By the nineteenth century, medical testing on live animals had become more widespread, and they were infected with diseases in an attempt to find treatments. Some people began to question the morality of using animals in this way, and societies campaigning for their better treatment were founded. In the United Kingdom, this led to the Cruelty to Animals Act of 1876, the first legislation that addressed animal experimentation. Under its terms animals had to be anaesthetized, while researchers had to be licensed and they could be prosecuted if they inflicted unnecessary pain.

The scientist most associated with the guinea pig is the German physician Robert Koch (1843–1910), whose work revolutionized the understanding of disease. In 1876, he identified the bacterium responsible for anthrax, and he then set out to understand one of the most lethal diseases of his day, tuberculosis. Popularly known as consumption, the disease infected the lungs and was epidemic in many cities, particularly in poor areas. Koch was certain tuberculosis was caused by a bacterium, which he identified as *Mycobacterium tuberculosis*. He tested his theory on guinea pigs, publishing his findings in 1882. Koch then worked on a cure for tuberculosis. He developed 'tuberculin', a liquid based on an extract from cultures of the tuberculosis bacterium. Tests on guinea pigs appeared positive and he announced his great success in 1890. This caused a global sensation, and Koch was hailed as a saviour, but it soon became clear his serum was ineffective in curing tuberculosis and it continued to be a serious threat to public health. There was some positive news: antitoxins (tested on guinea pigs and other animals) that treated the diseases tetanus and diphtheria were successfully developed. Tuberculosis was then brought under control in 1921, when a vaccine against it was developed. This was followed in 1951 by the invention of an effective treatment, the antibiotic isoniazid.

ZEBRAFISH

A member of the minnow family, the zebrafish is named for its striped body. Despite the fact it is a fish, it is widely used in human medical research, particularly drug development, modelling how diseases develop, and genetic studies. This is because 70 per cent of human genes can be found in zebrafish. They also breed quickly and their clear embryos mean scientists can monitor their development from conception.

By the early twentieth century, 'guinea pig' began to be used as a metaphor for the subject of an experiment. Aside from their temperament, the reason why guinea pigs had been so widely used was because their immune systems are broadly similar to a human's. Since the mid-twentieth century, their use in medical testing has declined, as researchers generally began to prefer mice and rats, largely because of their lower cost and higher reproduction rate. Guinea pigs continue to be used, albeit in smaller numbers, for animal testing. As the structure of their ear is similar to a human's, they are studied to better understand hearing, while their respiratory system's sensitivity to allergens means they are often used to find treatments for breathing problems.

Objections to subjecting animals to experimentation have been raised for centuries. It was argued that it caused animals unnecessary pain and suffering and that it was ethically unjust to use them for scientific research. Since the 1970s, the animal rights movement has gathered pace. Its proponents argue that animals have a right to live with dignity and respect. Opponents to this say that the benefits of medical testing on animals outweigh any negatives, and that they do not have the same rights as humans. Animals continue to be the subject of testing, although in most countries there is legislation in place that sets standards of hygiene for the conditions they are kept in, and requires that any suffering should be minimized.

Clever Hans the Horse

The question as to whether an animal can be taught to speak and understand human language has been long debated. Parrots have been taught to mimic human phrases, sometimes building up vocabularies of hundreds of words and in some cases even answering questions. Although great apes struggle to mimic human speech because of the structure of their tongue, jaw and vocal cords, several have been taught sign language, building up vocabularies of hundreds of words. However, many scientists question the degree to which this can truly be called 'language', and how much the animal actually understands. Likewise, the cognitive ability of animals has also been the subject of experimentation and conjecture. Can animals truly think and learn, or are they merely showing instinct, or responding to conditioning or training? The example of 'Clever Hans' shows the difficulty of accurately gauging if animals are truly capable of human-level thinking and communication.

Wilhelm von Osten (d. 1909) was a German secondary school mathematics teacher. He believed that people had undervalued the mental abilities of animals, and to prove his hunch he decided to try to teach mathematics to one. Attempts with a cat and a bear ended in failure, so he moved on to a stallion called Hans (who was an Orlov Trotter, a Russian breed). Von Osten started by teaching Hans to recognize numbers written on a chalkboard by tapping his hoof the requisite number of times. He then moved on to mathematical symbols (even the square root), and giving the answers to equations. Next was the alphabet. Hans would tap his foot to correspond to a different letter; one tap meant 'A', two meant 'B', and so forth. This opened up Hans's ability to spell out the names of composers whose music he was played, or the name of the artist when shown a painting. Hans also appeared to be able to recognize colours and playing cards, read a clock and answer questions about upcoming dates in the calendar. To show the public just how clever Hans was, in 1891, von Osten began holding free exhibitions of his talents in Berlin. The public were amazed; Hans answered questions with 90 per cent accuracy and seemed to have the mathematical ability of a fourteen-year-old.

Sceptics began to doubt von Osten, claiming he was somehow tipping off Hans. Sigmund Freud (1856–1939), the founder of psychoanalysis, suggested a telepathic relationship between Hans and von Osten was responsible. Even when von Osten was not present, and another trainer asked questions, Hans would still correctly tap out his answer with his hoof the vast majority of the time. The German Board of Education aimed to get to the bottom of the matter, and in 1904 ordered the formation of a commission to investigate Hans. It was headed by the philosopher and psychologist Carl Stumpf (1848–1936), who gathered zoologists, veterinarians, animal trainers, teachers and even a circus manager. After eighteen months of study, they declared von Osten was not perpetuating a hoax.

Evaluation continued under Oskar Pfungst (1874–1932), one of Stumpf's assistants at the University of Berlin. In 1907, after further investigation and experimentation, he found the explanation. Hans was responding to tiny cues in posture and facial expression from the questioner.

He would sense the minute changes that occurred after he had tapped his hoof the correct number of times, and stop tapping, thereby appearing to have given the correct answer. Pfungst proved this by having the questioner ask Hans something they did not know the answer to, or by screening off Hans. In both cases, because he had no visual cue to respond to, he would give the wrong answer. The riddle of 'Clever Hans' had been solved. Although he clearly had an impressive ability to respond to human body language, he could not be said to be truly answering the questions. As a result of the affair, it became best practice in experiments and research into animal communication to minimize face-to-face contact with the subject. This would ensure accurate results and avoid any false positives.

Although Hans's human-level mental abilities had been scientifically debunked, von Osten continued to display him in public, often attracting large crowds. Von Osten died in 1909, and Hans was sold on, going through a series of owners. When World War I broke out in 1914, many horses were volunteered for military service by their owners or requisitioned by the German government. Despite his celebrity, Hans was not exempt from military service. Sadly, he disappears from the official record in 1916, suggesting he was probably one of the millions of equine casualties of the conflict.

JIM THE HORSE

Diphtheria is a disease, most serious among children, caused by exposure to a bacterium. It can lead to breathing problems, fever and even death. In the 1890s, scientists created an antitoxin that treated it. They did this by injecting horses with the diphtheria bacterium, collecting their blood, and harvesting the antibodies fighting the infection to make into an injectable serum. Jim was an American horse who produced over 28 litres (49 pints) of serum but in 1901 contracted tetanus and was put down. However, contaminated serum from Jim had been distributed, leading to the deaths of thirteen children. This led to stricter regulation of pharmaceuticals.

MARTHA THE PASSENGER PIGEON

On 1 September 1914, a passenger pigeon called Martha died in her cage at Cincinnati Zoo. Bred in captivity, Martha often trembled as the result of a palsy and had never laid a fertile egg. She had been the last known member of her species for over four years. She attracted hundreds of visitors, who sometimes threw sand in her cage to encourage her to move about. Her death marked the extinction of the passenger pigeon, which had once been one of the most numerous bird species in the world.

The passenger pigeon was native to North America. Before the arrival of Europeans there, they once comprised over one-quarter of the bird population there, numbering between 3 and 5 billion. Their main breeding grounds were the forests that once covered much of eastern North America, and in the winter they migrated, mostly west, in search of food. Their name comes from the French *passager*, which means 'to pass by', and refers to their migratory habits. They lived and travelled in vast flocks, sometimes numbering into the millions, and were rapid flyers, reaching speeds of 95 kilometres per hour (almost 60 miles per hour). It was said that when a flock of passenger pigeons flew by they would block out the sun, and make so much noise it was impossible to conduct a conversation. Their nesting sites could be huge. One in Wisconsin was recorded as covering over 2,000 square kilometres (nearly 800 square miles) and hosting 136 million birds. Passenger pigeons roosted in trees, sometimes in such numbers that they broke their branches. Their dense populations meant predators could do little damage to the overall strength of their flock; even if a few birds or eggs were lost, the impact would be minimal.

By the early nineteenth century, the United States was expanding westward. Its cities, then mostly concentrated on the Eastern Seaboard, were rapidly growing in population, fuelled by migration from Europe. This came at the expense of the indigenous Native Americans, who suffered from violence and diseases brought by the settlers. The lands that they had lived, hunted and foraged in for centuries were claimed by settlers. In the process, thousands of square kilometres of forest were cut down, robbing passenger pigeons of their habitat.

Hunters posed the greatest threat to the passenger pigeon. Due to their dense populations, the birds were extremely straightforward to kill. Swinging a stick through a flock could easily bring down a handful of birds. Demand for meat from urban areas would transform the hunting of the passenger pigeon, and encourage commercialized mass killing on a vast scale. This was helped by innovations in transport and communication. The nationwide electrical telegraph network enabled reports of the movement of flocks to be spread rapidly, while the railways could be used to transport the birds (usually packed into barrels) quickly to market. Hunters would find nesting sites of the passenger pigeon and kill them by the thousand. A common technique was to start fires or light sulphur beneath trees they were nesting in, which would cause them to become dazed and fall to the ground. An alternative technique was simply to cut down trees they were nesting in, or bait with grain soaked in alcohol. Sometimes, captive passenger pigeons (or models) were set up as decoys on small perches, called 'stools'. This then attracted other passenger pigeons who flocked to the area thinking a member of their flock had found food – they were then trapped in a net. This practice gave rise to the term 'stool pigeon', for an informant who betrays their associates to the authorities.

By the 1860s and 1870s, the passenger pigeon was clearly in rapid decline, but the slaughter continued. In 1896, the last sizeable flock, numbering 250,000, was discovered – hunters killed all but a few. The last definite sighting of a wild passenger pigeon was in 1901; it was shot and stuffed. By this time, the federal government had finally been roused into action (although some states had already passed local laws to protect the passenger pigeon). The previous May, the Lacey Act was signed into law, the first national legislation passed in the United States that protected wildlife. It prohibited interstate trade of unlawfully killed game and fish (as well as plants illegally taken). Another law, passed in 1918, protected migratory birds. They came too late to help the passenger pigeon. Many continued to be kept in captivity, but attempts at breeding them ended in failure.

The passenger pigeon became symbolic of the vulnerability to extinction of even seemingly healthy species, and the necessity of protecting wildlife from human exploitation. Scientists have harvested DNA from surviving specimens and used it to model the passenger pigeon's genome. Gaps were filled using DNA from its nearest living relative, the band-tailed pigeon. This has raised the possibility of one day bringing back the passenger pigeon, but it is unknown if this would be successful, given its predilection to flock in extremely large numbers.

As for Martha, after she died she was frozen into a 140-kilogram (over 300 pounds) block of ice and dispatched by train to the Smithsonian in Washington, D.C. She was dissected, stuffed and then exhibited at the National Museum of Natural History until 1999, when she was removed from permanent public display.

Black Rats

. . . .

On 15 June 1918, the steamship *Makambo* ran aground on Lord Howe Island, 780 kilometres (480 miles) northeast of Sydney. Lord Howe Island, which had remained undiscovered by humans until the later eighteenth century, was home to many unique species of plants, birds and insects. Lurking amid the *Makambo*'s cargo of fruits and vegetables was a threat to this biodiversity: the black rat. The *Makambo* was refloated and went on with its voyage (it was later sold to a Japanese company and sunk by a British submarine in 1944), but not before some black rats scurried ashore. Lacking any natural predators, the black rats flourished, but at a severe cost to the flora and fauna of Lord Howe Island. They caused the extinction of five species of birds, thirteen species of insects and two plants that could be found nowhere else. During the 1920s, Tasmanian masked owls were introduced to the island to control the black rats but they caused even more damage to the local avian population and also seabirds who nested there. What happened on Lord Howe Island is a microcosm of how the black rat, and related species of rats, have become invasive and caused severe damage to local wildlife. This has been going on for millennia, but accelerated in the past five centuries as a result of the rise of global maritime trade and European imperialism and colonialism.

The black rat probably originated in South East Asia, spreading from there into India. Carried overland, it reached the Arabian Peninsula by 2000 BC, Palestine by 1000 BC and the western Mediterranean by 400 BC. By the time the black rat arrived in Britain during the third century AD, it was well established across Eurasia and North Africa. In the ninth century, Arab traders introduced black rats to islands in the Indian Ocean, and from the sixteenth century they began to spread into the Americas, carried across the Atlantic on European ships.

One reason for their ubiquity is that black rats breed extremely quickly; they reach sexual maturity at two to four months and within a year a breeding pair could produce 10,000 descendants. Black rats are also omnivorous and opportunistic foragers with a strong sense of smell, as well as being highly agile and an adept swimmer. This makes them ideally suited to living near human settlement. They can eat grains and fruits cultivated by farmers and, as they eat almost anything digestible, waste produced in urban areas provides another ample food source. They are just as comfortable in uninhabited areas, as they can scurry up to and through treetops in search of food, particularly juvenile birds and eggs. The spread of the black rat has had negative implications for humans; they damaged crops and helped to spread disease, most seriously plague.

Rabbits

Native to south-western Europe and north-western Africa, the rabbit had been deliberately introduced to the rest of Europe by the medieval period. From the later eighteenth century, British colonists brought rabbits to Australia, New Zealand and many Pacific islands, where they were hunted as a game animal or used as a food source for sailors. Like rats, rabbits became invasive and caused serious damage to these ecosystems. Their burrowing led to soil erosion and their grazing wreaked havoc among native plants and agricultural crops.

Humans have spread two other species of rat worldwide. The first is the Polynesian rat, which, like the black rat, also originated in South East Asia. When humans began to settle the islands of the Pacific, from 3000 BC on, they carried the Polynesian rat with them. This may have been partly deliberate, as it was sometimes eaten and its fur was used to make clothing. The second is the brown rat, which came from northern China and had reached Europe by the mid-fifteenth century. It spread to Britain around 1720, just as it was about to embark on two centuries of imperialist expansion, allowing it to spread across the world. Larger and more aggressive than the black rat, it supplanted it in many areas, particularly in more temperate environments.

Black rats were most successful in more tropical environments, particularly islands where they had no natural predators. During the nineteenth and twentieth centuries, islands that were once remote, particularly in the Pacific, became part of a global shipping network. What happened on Lord Howe Island was repeated in thousands of other places. As blacks rats are able to swim distances of 300 to 750 metres (1,000 to 2,500 feet), this meant they could colonize nearby islands. Consequently, only small and uninhabited islands tend to be rat-free. Tropical islands presented a range of food sources for black rats: birds, reptiles, spiders, insects, crustaceans, turtles; all were eaten, contributing to numerous extinctions. The black rat's preferred food source, though, is plant matter.

Their feeding on seeds and fruits interrupts pollination. Together with their propensity to eat buds and gnaw on bark, this means black rats can seriously damage forests. In doing so, this disrupts the food supply of other animals, as well as destroying their habitat. Black rats survive in even the least promising environments – they do not even need a source of fresh water, as they can get all the water they need from dew, rainfall and moisture in their food. Black rats even continued to survive on Eniwetok Atoll after the Americans used it as a testing ground for nuclear weapons, detonating forty-three bombs there from 1948 to 1958.

There have been efforts to rid areas of their invasive rat populations. For the most part, this has only been possible on smaller islands. The largest place it has been done is South Georgia, an island in the South Atlantic Ocean around 3,500 square kilometres (1,400 square miles) in size, which was declared rat-free in 2018. This was achieved by dumping 300,000 kilograms (300 tons) of poison across the island, killing its population of black rats. Such methods show the drastic actions that might have to be considered if humans wish to rid environments of black rats and other invasive species.

Tigers

. . . .

The largest living species of cat, tigers first evolved 2 million years ago. Their historical range once extended across most of Asia, from Anatolia to the shores of the East China Sea, and as far south as Bali in Indonesia. Tigers are thus comfortable in many environments, from the freezing taiga (snowy forests) to dry grassland to tropical rainforest. Wherever they live, tigers are apex predators, hunting nocturnally, seeking to ambush prey like boar, deer and elk. Apart from mothers and cubs (who remain together for two to three years), tigers are mostly solitary. They are also highly territorial, and a single tiger can have a home range of up to 4,000 square kilometres (1,500 square miles). Tigers have branched into various regional subspecies. The largest is the Siberian tiger, which lives mainly in the Russian Far East, as well as parts of Northeast China and possibly the far north of North Korea. It measures up to 4 metres (13 feet) and weighs 300 kilograms (650 pounds). Like other tigers, it has orange-brown fur with dark stripes. However, the Siberian tiger tends to have longer, thicker, softer and paler fur, with extra growth around its paws to protect it from the snow.

Across Asia, tigers have been the subject of veneration and respect for millennia. In India, tigers are symbolic of power and bravery, and one of them is the vehicle of Durga, the Hindu goddess of war. Although the tiger has now disappeared from most of the Korean Peninsula, it was once revered as a deity of the mountains and a sacred guardian, and stone tigers guard royal tombs of the Joseon dynasty, which ruled Korea from 1391 to 1910. Tigers still play a talismanic protective role in its culture, and were symbols of national unity and resistance during its time under Japanese rule (1910–45). The Siberian tiger is the national animal of South Korea and one was the mascot of the 1988 Seoul Olympics. In China, the tiger represents masculinity, and is seen as ruler of the animals because the four stripes on its head resemble the character *wáng*, which means 'king'. Given this, it is no wonder that when East Asian countries began to undergo rapid industrialization and growth in prosperity from the 1950s and 1960s, they began to be known as 'tiger economies'. Despite the respect for tigers, their numbers have steadily declined, particularly since the beginning of the twentieth century, leaving them on the point of extinction.

In 1900, there were around 100,000 tigers left in the wild. By 2015, there were just 3,200 left. Many subspecies had become extinct, such as the Caspian, Javan and Bali tigers.

In addition, the South China tiger may have disappeared in the wild. This leaves just five subspecies of tiger: the Siberian, Bengal, Indochinese, Malayan and Sumatran. There were many causes for this precipitous decline. Firstly, tigers were a much-desired target for hunters, who saw them as the ultimate prey. Secondly, their pelts were in demand for clothing and decoration. Thirdly, almost every part of the tiger is seen as a potentially powerful ingredient in traditional Chinese medicine, and believed to combat a range of ailments. Their ground-up bones are used to treat arthritis, while their blood is thought to build willpower, and even their bile is believed to prevent convulsions in children. Finally, and most importantly, the tiger lost habitat as a result of pollution, rising populations, farming and logging. This robbed tigers not just of their territory but of the animals they hunted. Indeed, the Siberian tiger's habitat was so diminished that it no longer lives in the region it is named after. For this reason, it is sometimes called the Amur tiger, after the river that runs through its remaining range.

During the twentieth century, thousands of tigers were captured for public display. There are now more tigers in captivity than in the wild. They are particularly widespread in the United States, where there may be up to 10,000 captive tigers. Only a minority are held in zoos; many are kept in private homes. The keeping of tigers in captivity is largely unregulated, and they suffer from abuse, neglect and inbreeding. Many cubs are killed when they become too big to handle. The keeping and breeding of tigers in captivity does not truly equate to conservation because there is almost no way they can return to the wild. Even more problematically, tigers are often bred with lions to produce 'ligers' and 'tigons'; these animals suffer from neurological issues and genetic defects.

In recent decades, tiger numbers have begun to make a slow recovery, and as of 2020 there were around 3,900 in the wild, about half of which are Bengals living in India. This means that tiger numbers are rising for the first time in over a century. Governments have moved to prohibit products, particularly medical ones, made of tigers, and in 1997 international trade in tiger parts was banned. Areas have been set aside as tiger sanctuaries, and poaching and hunting of them has been clamped down on. Russia's Far East, a remote and sparsely populated region, represents the largest continuous tiger habitat. It is home to over 500 Siberian tigers, a huge increase from the 1940s, when there were no more than thirty left. There are concerted efforts to ensure that their numbers remain stable. Their population is closely monitored by cameras and tagging, and orphaned cubs are rehabilitated until they can survive in the wild. The story of the recovery of the Siberian tiger, and other tiger subspecies, shows that even the most majestic animals can disappear from the wild, but that with concerted effort, recovery from the brink of extinction is possible.

LAIKA THE DOG

After World War II, two superpowers remained: the United States and the Soviet Union. Their Cold War lasted for over half a century. Both nations vied for supremacy without directly entering into conflict. One of the most significant theatres of their rivalry was space, which would catapult a stray dog from Moscow to global fame.

The space race was not an idealistic quest for scientific discovery. Rather, it was subsumed into an ideological struggle for dominance. Gaining the upper hand would not only provide a public symbol of technological superiority, but have military implications. This was because rockets would be a potentially unstoppable delivery system for nuclear weapons. Both the Americans and Soviets harboured ambitions of manned space flight, but, as its effects on living beings were unknown, animals would be sent up first. The Americans initiated this by launching fruit flies in 1947, followed by monkeys and chimpanzees. The Soviets experimented with mice, rats and rabbits, but their most commonly used animal cosmonauts were dogs.

The Soviets primarily used dogs because they were trainable and easy to procure. Strays were preferred because it was believed life on the streets had prepared them for the rigours of their training. Candidates had to be small enough to fit in capsules and have lighter coats that would show up on film. Only females would be selected because they would be more placid, and it was easier to design space suits for them because they did not have to raise their leg to urinate. Dozens of dogs were gathered; they were trained to live in progressively smaller cages for up to twenty days and to eat jellied food. They were subjected to loud noises and changes in pressure as well as being spun in centrifuges. Dogs were sent up in pairs so their experiences could be compared – the first two were Dezik and Tsygan, who in 1951 survived a suborbital flight that reached an altitude of 109 kilometres (68 miles).

On 4 October 1957, the Soviets sent the first artificial satellite into Earth orbit: Sputnik 1 (which meant 'fellow traveller'). The Soviet leader, Nikita Khrushchev (1894–1971), ordered this be followed up with a satellite containing the first animal to go into orbit. This had to be done in just over a month, to coincide with the fortieth anniversary of the October Revolution, which had seen the Communists win power in Russia. Soviet scientists did not have time to design a capsule that would return to Earth, and nor would it be big enough for two dogs. Rather, Sputnik 2 was a one-way trip for a single mongrel called Laika (whose name meant 'Barker').

Before Laika's mission, one of the scientists took her home to play with his children, hoping to give her a final happy experience. A device was implanted in Laika that allowed her blood pressure, breathing rate and heartbeat to be monitored. Laika was then flown to Baikonur Cosmodrome, the Soviet space-launch facility in Kazakhstan, and three days before take-off was placed in her capsule. Sputnik 2 was launched on 3 November 1957. As she was sent hurtling into space, Laika's heart rate tripled and her breathing rate quadrupled. It took over three hours for them to reach normal levels, and, while weightless, she ate some of her food. By this time, Sputnik 2, and Laika, were orbiting the Earth. Not all was going to plan. The thermal control system was not operating correctly, meaning temperatures in Laika's capsule rose to over 37 degrees Celsius. During her fourth orbit, five to seven hours into the mission, Laika died of a combination of overheating and panic. Sputnik 2 fell back to Earth on 14 April 1958, burning up in the atmosphere, meaning Laika's remains were lost. The Soviet leadership hid the circumstances of Laika's death, claiming she had died after six to seven days as a result of lack of oxygen – the truth was not revealed until 2002.

After Sputnik 2, the Soviets enjoyed more success in space. In 1960, two dogs, Belka and Strelka, accompanied by mice, rats, a rabbit and fruit flies, safely returned after an orbital flight. It was not until the following April that Yuri Gagarin (1934–68) became the first human to do the same thing. Later that year, Khrushchev sent one of Strelka's puppies, Pushinka ('Fluffy'), to President John F. Kennedy (1917–63). The presentation was a diplomatic gesture but also a subtle reminder of Soviet space supremacy – at that time the Americans had not yet sent a human into orbit. Pushinka would have four puppies of her own with another presidential dog, a Welsh terrier called Charlie, before being given away to a White House gardener after Kennedy was assassinated in 1963. In the years after Kennedy's death, the American space programme gained the ascendancy over the Soviets, and in 1969 completed his ambitious plan of sending men to the moon by the end of the decade. However, the achievements of both the Americans and Soviets in space would have been impossible without the sacrifices of animals like Laika.

No. 65

On 31 January 1961, NASA launched 'No. 65' into suborbital flight. During his mission, which lasted sixteen minutes and thirty-nine seconds, he pulled a lever in response to a flashing light, showing it was possible to complete tasks in space. 'No. 65' was a three-year-old chimpanzee, who was renamed 'Ham' after he returned to Earth.

DAVID GREYBEARD THE CHIMPANZEE

Until the 1960s, it was generally believed that humans were the only species to make and use tools; setting us apart from other animals and helping form the basis for our dominance over the natural world. This assumption was proved wrong thanks to the observation of a chimpanzee known as David Greybeard.

The first human species to use tools was *Homo habilis* (meaning 'handy man'), which evolved between 2.4 and 1.5 million years ago. Its fossils were first discovered in 1960 by a British scientific expedition to the Olduvai Gorge, an archaeological site in Tanzania where numerous early human remains have been uncovered, proving that modern humans had evolved in sub-Saharan Africa. Olduvai also yielded numerous examples of the stone tools early humans used to chop and crush animal carcasses and plants. The digs at Olduvai were led by the Kenyan-born anthropologist Louis Leakey (1903–72); in his quest to find out how humans had evolved, he wanted to uncover more about the behaviour of our closest ancestors, the great apes. To understand them, their way of life had to be observed in the wild – the person he settled on to do this was an Englishwoman called Jane Goodall (b. 1934).

Goodall had a passion for learning about animals but no formal scientific training at that point; she had travelled to Kenya in 1957. While there she contacted Leakey, who hired her as a secretary. He then proposed that she observe chimpanzee behaviour, and won a grant to pay for an expedition. She was the first of the 'Trimates': women Leakey selected to observe apes in the wild – the others were Dian Fossey (1932–85) and Birutė Galdikas (b. 1946), who studied, respectively, gorillas in Rwanda and orangutans in Borneo. Goodall's studies would be conducted in western Tanzania, in Gombe Stream Game Reserve, a 150-square-kilometre (58 square miles) area of forested valley and ridges on the eastern shore of Lake Tanganyika, inhabited by a range of wildlife including numerous chimpanzees. She arrived there on 14 July 1960, along with her mother, guides and a cook.

Up to this point there had been very few attempts to study chimpanzees and other apes in the wild. Goodall's initial weeks at Gombe showed the perils of this approach. Even when she went out alone, every time she got to within 500 metres (550 yards) of chimpanzees, they scattered. Although Goodall could observe the chimpanzees from a distance, she could make little progress in truly understanding their society (to make matters worse, she also suffered from a bout of malaria). After three months, the chimpanzees became familiar with Goodall and she was able to move closer to them. Goodall was able to recognize individuals. She named one of them David Greybeard, after the silvery hairs on his chin. On 30 October 1960, she observed him eating meat. This was a major discovery – up to that point it was believed chimpanzees were herbivores. Later, Goodall saw that chimpanzees frequently ate meat, killing monkeys, bush pigs and bushbucks (a species of antelope), as well as practising cannibalism.

Five days later, Goodall made an even more important discovery: chimpanzees could use tools. That day, she saw

David Greybeard and another, the alpha male of his band, Goliath, poking grass stalks into a termite mound. When pulled out, the stalks were covered with the insects, which they then sucked off. Later, she would see that chimpanzees would pull leaves off twigs for this purpose, and even carry them between termite mounds. This behaviour was not instinctual, but based on observing other chimpanzees doing it. It was a groundbreaking observation: humans were no longer the only animals that made and used tools. In other locations, chimpanzees would be observed using other tools, such as rocks to crush nuts and leaves to scoop up water.

In March 1961, David Greybeard began to appear regularly at Goodall's camp to feed on the ripe pine nuts that grew on a tree in the vicinity. One day, he approached the tents and swiped a banana that had been left out. To encourage him to return, more bananas were left out. He eventually grew comfortable enough to take a banana from Goodall's hand, and if they saw each other in the forest, he would greet her, showing familiarity. David Greybeard would also bring two members of his band to the camp: Goliath and William. This allowed Goodall to see that each one had a distinct personality: David Greybeard was calm, gentle and comforting, while Goliath was more aggressive and volatile, and William tended to be submissive and passive. All three grew used to Goodall, but none were as comfortable with her as David Greybeard.

Goodall, who was awarded her doctorate from the University of Cambridge in 1966 (despite having no undergraduate degree), would frequently return to Gombe over the decades. Her work there made her a global celebrity and redefined how people viewed chimpanzees. David Greybeard, the one who had done so much to help Goodall understand the species, died of pneumonia in 1968. Six years later, the chimpanzees had split into two communities and violent conflict broke out between them. The 'war' lasted until 1978, with one side vanquishing the other by killing all ten of their males, including Goliath. For all that chimpanzees can mirror humanity's ingenuity and compassion, they also reveal our darker side of violence and rancour.

Bottlenose Dolphins

Dolphins are among the most intelligent of animals, with the ability to problem-solve, mimic and learn quickly. They also have highly advanced communication skills, as well as being self-aware and capable of showing empathy and experiencing emotions that could be characterized as grief.

Bottlenose dolphins are highly social, living in 'pods' that range in size from a couple to over 1,000 for hunting when prey is abundant. Membership of these groups is dynamic, changing frequently. Groups of females live with their calves in pods of five to twenty. Males will form pairs or trios that can persist for decades. These can then form temporary alliances with other groups to defend or steal females for mating. To deal with their highly fluid social world, bottlenose dolphins have a highly developed paralimbic system (the part of the brain that deals with emotion and behaviour). They will care for sick or wounded members of their pod, for example helping them to the surface of the water so they can breathe. They communicate with each other using a series of whistles, screams and clicks, as well as using body language like slapping their tail on the water. They may also show aggression by clapping their jaws together or exhaling rapidly through their blowhole. Each bottlenose dolphin has a unique 'signature' whistle that others recognize, even after up to twenty years apart. This suggests that, aside from humans, they have the longest memory of any animal.

Observation of the hunting habits of bottlenose dolphins shows their cognitive abilities and cooperation.

One technique is for groups to form a line and then force fish onto the shore, before half-beaching to grab them out of the surf and slide back into the water. They will also trap schools of fish against sandbars or sea walls. Bottlenose dolphins in Australia have been seen using sponges to protect their beaks as they dig into the sand, hoping to scare up fish that live on the seabed. Females tend to display more innovative hunting practices because they have to find additional food to feed their calves. When they are hunting, bottlenose dolphins use echolocation, emitting rapid high-pitched clicks that bounce off underwater objects. By listening to the reflected sound, they can determine what and where the object is, as well as the speed and direction of its travel.

Many scientists have attempted to find a way to

communicate with dolphins. They have been trained to respond to vocal and verbal cues from humans, and analysis of their speech has led some researchers to claim it may be advanced enough to be akin to human language. One of the thinkers who was most convinced that dolphins could be communicated with was the American scientist John Lilly (1915–2001). During the 1950s and 1960s, he came to believe it was possible to teach dolphins to mimic human speech. As part of his research, Lilly opened an institute in the US Virgin Islands to study human–dolphin communication. It housed three bottlenose dolphins and received funding from NASA, which was interested in finding techniques of communicating with non-human species in the event of contact with extraterrestrial life forms. In 1965, a volunteer at the centre, Margaret Howe Lovatt (b. 1942), spent six months living with one of the dolphins, Peter, in a flooded room in an attempt to teach him to speak using his blowhole. The project ended the next year when funding ran out. Peter, who had grown extremely close to Howe Lovatt, was moved to a facility in Miami that had inadequate space and little sunlight. Tragically, he committed suicide by refusing to continue breathing and sinking to the bottom of his tank and suffocating.

Some nations have sought to harness the dolphin's

intelligence for their militaries. Since the 1960s, the US Navy has been training bottlenose dolphins (as well as sea lions) to find and retrieve objects at sea and identify potentially hostile swimmers approaching ships. During the Vietnam War, bottlenose dolphins were deployed to patrol around ships, and in 2003 some were flown to ships stationed off southern Iraq to help locate mines in the Persian Gulf. In 2012, the US Navy announced it would replace its animals with robots. As of yet this has not happened because none of the robotic prototypes have been able to match the performance of the animals. In addition, both Russia and Ukraine may also be using dolphins and other marine mammals for naval operations.

Such programmes have attracted criticism for being exploitative, but they pale in comparison to how dolphins, and many other aquatic animals, are treated in water parks. As of 2019, over 3,000 dolphins (mostly bottlenose dolphins) are held in captivity worldwide. Many are held in tanks, either alone or in small groups, where they are trained to perform tricks for audiences and submit to guests swimming with them and touching them. Such conditions can cause significant stress and health problems for captive dolphins, as they are used to swimming long distances in deep water, interacting with many other dolphins, and hunting for wild, live prey. The precise nature of the dolphin's intelligence and cognitive ability may still not be fully understood, but the trauma inflicted on these inquisitive and complex animals is clear.

AN AQUATIC HEIR?

Guigues IV of Albon (d. 1142) was a medieval French noble. As he sported a dolphin on his coat of arms, he and his successors were known as *le Dauphin*. In 1349, his descendant Humbert II of Viennois (1312–55), who had no surviving children and severe financial troubles, sold the family's lands, an area known as the Dauphiné, to the King of France. Humbert stipulated that all future heirs apparent to the French throne should bear the title Dauphin. This tradition continued, albeit with an interlude during the Revolutionary and Napoleonic periods, until 1830.

FROGS

. . . .

The *Anura* order of animals, better known as frogs, are amphibians that are usually found in water, although some live on land and even in trees. They predominately eat insects but some eat worms, rodents, reptiles or other frogs. There are over 6,000 extant species of frog; most of them are smooth-skinned and can move by leaping. Those species that are squat, warty and hop are often known as 'toads', but this is an informal distinction. Frogs have protruding eyes, no necks, webbed hind feet and, apart from two species found in North America, are tailless.

Most frogs (and other amphibians) have permeable skin, which they use to directly absorb oxygen and water. To prevent it drying out, the skin is covered with glands that secrete a slimy mucus. This covers their body and prevents many bacteria, viruses and fungi from entering it. As well as helping the frog to maintain its health, these secretions make the frog slippery and thus harder for predators to catch and eat them. In some species of frog, the substances are toxic – sometimes extremely so. The poison frogs, which live in the tropical forests of Central and South America, are the most lethal. Like many other frogs, they have brightly coloured skin that serves to warn predators of their toxicity, or perhaps even confuse them. Indigenous peoples in these areas were said to have rubbed their arrow tips onto the backs of these frogs when hunting. The golden poison frog, which lives in Colombia, is the most lethal. Bright yellow and only 5 centimetres (2 inches) long, just one of them can kill ten adults. Their secretions contain a poison called batrachotoxin – if ingested, it embeds itself in the proteins that conduct electrical impulses along nerves and muscles before disrupting them, ultimately causing death through paralysis and heart attack.

Since the mid-twentieth century, antibiotics, which can kill or prevent the growth of a wide range of bacterial infections, have saved hundreds of millions of lives. However, overuse has led to some bacteria developing resistance to antibiotics (such as Methicillin-resistant *Staphylococcus aureus*, better known as MRSA). This threatens to undermine one of the foundations of public health in the twenty-first century. As such, finding novel treatments for bacteria is crucial. Frogs may provide a useful avenue for future research, as their skin contains natural antibiotic properties that mean they can swim in bacteria-filled water without wounds becoming infected. For example, the skin of the foothill yellow-legged frog, which is native to western North America, may be useful in combatting MRSA. Somewhat paradoxically, some of the most dangerous frogs are the source of potentially highly valuable new medical treatments. The secretions of poison frogs could be used to make powerful painkillers, as well as muscle relaxants and anaesthetics.

The African clawed frog, found across much of sub-Saharan Africa, is the source of a technology that could revolutionize medicine: the xenobot, which was invented in 2020. Xenobots, so-called because the Latin name for the African clawed frog is *Xenopus laevis*, are synthetic organisms that measure less than 1 millimetre (0.04 inches). They are made from the skin and heart muscle stem cells of the embryos of African clawed frogs. While the skin cells hold the xenobot together, the pulsing of the heart allows them to move. Their shape is based on a complex computer algorithm that uses a process of trial and error to design them. Xenobots have been programmed to carry and push things, and can work both independently and in groups. They can heal themselves and survive for weeks at a time. It is hoped that in the future they could be used to deliver medicine inside the body, as well as clear plaque from arteries. Even more promisingly, they may have applications in removing microplastics from the ocean or clearing up after toxic spills.

There is a major threat to the existence of the

world's frogs (and other amphibians): a fungus called *Batrachochytrium dendrobatidis* (*Bd*). It exists as a waterborne fungal spore that infects the skin of a frog, where it grows and germinates, producing more spores. In the process, it degrades their skin, eventually causing death by heart attack. The fungus is particularly difficult to combat because it can 'swim' a short distance and live outside the skin for weeks or even months. Also, it takes several days to cause death, meaning infected amphibians have longer to spread it. *Bd* was first discovered in 1998 but it has been causing amphibian deaths worldwide since at least the 1970s. Recent studies have shown that it probably originated in Korea, where the local amphibians have developed a resistance to it. It may have started in the aftermath of the Korean War (1950–3), when soldiers returning home unwittingly carrying infected amphibians in their weapons and equipment. These amphibians then introduced diseases that caused havoc in a population that had not built up a resistance to it. Furthermore, the development of a global market for pet amphibians added to the spread of *Bd*. There are now outbreaks of *Bd*, and similar fungal infections, across the Americas, Europe, Australia and Africa. Although fungicides can treat the infection, these cannot be readily applied to wild amphibians, making *Bd* a dire threat. It has already caused the extinction of around a hundred amphibian species. As a result, over 30 per cent of those that remain are in decline. Frogs and other amphibians thus could be on the verge of a mass dying-out, potentially on a par with the extinction of the dinosaurs.

ATLANTIC HORSESHOE CRABS

Limulus amebocyte lysate (LAL) is used to test bacterial contamination in medical treatments and equipment. Its only known natural source is the blood of the Atlantic horseshoe crab (actually more closely related to ticks, spiders and scorpions), a 'living fossil' unchanged for around 445 million years. Every year, thousands of them are gathered, bled and released – in the process many die, leaving them vulnerable to extinction. Recent conservation efforts, as well as the development of a synthetic version of LAL in 2003, should help to preserve them.

DOLLY THE SHEEP

. . . .

Humans have been selectively breeding animals (and plants) for millennia. Cloning represents the apex of this effort to breed specimens with the most valuable traits, and offers powerful solutions to ecological and health problems, while at the same time posing ethical issues. The animal who captured the benefits and dangers of this technology was Dolly the Sheep, the first mammal to be successfully cloned from an adult cell.

By around 8000 BC, sheep, following dogs, had become the second animal to be domesticated. Descended from the wild mouflon, the sheep was domesticated in Mesopotamia. It was raised for its milk, meat and skins, but it was perhaps its fleece that made it such a popular breed. By the Bronze Age, wool was being spun into yarn, which was then weaved into textiles. Few animals are as efficient at converting grazing land into clothing and meat as sheep, and for this reason there are now over 1 billion of them in the world.

Located near Edinburgh, the Roslin Institute was formally established in 1993 to conduct research into animal biology (it traces its origins back to the University of Edinburgh's Institute of Animal Genetics, founded in 1919, which officially became part of the university in 2008). One of its main foci was on farm animals, and improving their health and productivity through selective breeding. It was as part of this mission that Dolly the Sheep came to life in 1996. She was the first mammal cloned from an adult cell; born as part of a project, led by Professor Sir Ian Wilmut (b. 1944), that aimed to breed animals whose milk contains proteins that can be used to treat human diseases.

Before Dolly, creating clones from adult animal cells of more complex species was thought impossible (although it had been done in frogs). This is because once cells become fully differentiated into a specific function (for example an organ, skin or muscles), they lose their ability to become any other type of cell. Previously, it was believed that only cells from embryos were able to grow into any type of cell. Indeed, Wilmut's team had not even been trying to make clones from adult cells. Rather, they had been using foetal cells to make clones and had used the adult ones only as a control group.

Dolly began life as '6LL3'. She was created from cells harvested from the mammary glands of a six-year-old Finn Dorset sheep. To stop the cells growing and dividing, they were starved by being placed in a low-nutrient culture. These cells were then placed inside an unfertilized 'host egg' (from which the nucleus had been removed) that had been taken from another breed of sheep, the Scottish Blackface. Mild electrical pulses were then used to fuse the mammary cell with the host egg and encourage it to resume dividing. This process, called somatic cell nuclear transfer (SCNT), created 277 embryos, which were then transferred into thirteen surrogate ewes. Only one became pregnant, giving birth to Dolly on 5 July 1996 (named after the country music icon Dolly Parton). Dolly was announced to the public on 22 February 1997. She created a media storm, and became an instant celebrity.

Dolly continued to live at the Roslin Institute and had six lambs with a Welsh mountain ram. She suffered from arthritis, which may have been due to her spending a long time in a shed with a concrete floor (for security reasons) as well as growing overweight due to being fed treats so she would pose for photos. On 10 February 2003, it was discovered that Dolly had a cough – four days later, a scan showed she had lung tumours and it was decided to put her to sleep to spare her any future suffering. Dolly was just six (the normal lifespan of a sheep is about ten years). Her body was donated to the National Museum of Scotland in Edinburgh, where it remains on display.

Since Dolly, several other mammal species have been cloned using SNCT, including pigs, cats, deer, horses, dogs, wolves, mice and macaques. In 2008, scientists in California announced that they had cloned five human embryos through SCNT, but they did not implant them into wombs. SCNT does not require cells harvested from a living specimen, raising hopes it could be used to bring back extinct species. In 2003, SCNT was used to clone a Pyrenean ibex, a breed of wild goat that had become extinct three years previously – unfortunately, it died of a lung defect after a few minutes. It appears unlikely that SCNT will be able to be used to revive long-extinct species as it requires a fully intact cell nucleus, which is often unavailable.

The method used to create Dolly proved to be time-consuming and inefficient. For one, cloned embryos are much more likely to be lost during pregnancy and suffer from birth defects. Cloning has now been superseded by gene editing, which can add valuable traits and remove undesirable ones. This has been most successfully achieved using an enzyme from DNA called CRISPR-Cas9, discovered in 2012, which can 'cut' strands of other DNA. This means that certain genes in DNA can be made inactive as well as allowing new genes (even from other animals) to be added. In animals, it has been used to create cows with increased resistance to bovine tuberculosis, cure liver disease in rats, and eliminate muscular dystrophy in mice, and in the future it may have powerful applications for human use.

Dolly proved revolutionary because she showed that adult DNA had all the material needed to produce another animal. Inspired by her, a team in Japan developed induced pluripotent stem cells, adult cells reprogrammed to be as useful as embryonic cells (extensively used to replace dying or defective cells). This discovery created the possibility of harvesting cells from a patient, creating stem cells from them, and then using them to reset the normal function of cells, thereby treating conditions like Alzheimer's or Parkinson's. Dolly also unleashed a wave of debate about the morality of cloning. In many countries there are strict guidelines about cloning that allow it only to be used for scientific research. There were, and are, major concerns about how it could be used to manufacture human life, and in 2005 the United Nations issued a non-binding declaration against cloning people. Whatever the future of the manipulation or reproduction of DNA, human or otherwise, Dolly the Sheep played a major role in pushing forward the boundaries of science.

MONTAUCIEL THE SHEEP

On 19 September 1783, the Montgolfier brothers launched the first flight of their hot-air balloon with living beings as passengers; joining a duck and a rooster was a sheep called Montauciel ('Climb-to-the-sky'). All of the animals survived the eight-minute flight, travelling 450 metres (1,500 feet high), proving it was safe for humans to ascend into the skies.

5

TRADE AND INDUSTRY

BEES

. . . .

Humans have strived to control and regulate the natural world to their benefit for thousands of years. However, the flourishing of countless plant species, both wild and domesticated, is predicated on the diligent toil of the bee. Indeed, over one-quarter of the food we grow is pollinated by bees.

Millions of years ago, when seed plants first evolved, the pollen from the males was scattered into the air and only by chance would the wind blow it onto a female. This was an inefficient and wasteful process. Fortunately for plants, their pollen was highly nutritious and eaten by a range of animals, particularly insects. Although they consumed much of the pollen, some of it would be spread to other flowers as they flew around. As such, plants evolved to appeal more to insects, becoming more distinctive by developing colourful flowers that stood out amid other vegetation. They also produced a sugar-rich liquid called nectar to further encourage insects to feed on their pollen. The animal that evolved to take full advantage of the nutritional bounty offered by plants was the bee.

Bees evolved from wasps, around 130 million years ago,

in Asia. They are wholly dependent on plants for food, feeding on pollen and honey (which is nectar they modify). They developed long tongues (some reaching over 2.5 centimetres [1 inch]) that they use to suck nectar out of plants, as well as hairy bodies and legs that pollen clings to. This means that when bees fly from flower to flower they help them breed by propagating their pollen. Bees have excellent eyesight (they can distinguish between colours) and two odour-detecting antennae. Some species use a form of dancing to communicate to other bees information about the presence, size, distance and quality of flowers. There are now over 20,000 species of bee.

Despite their reputation for living in hives, the first bees were solitary. The majority of extant bee species remain this way and live in nests, which they sometimes create by burrowing into the ground. Solitary bees, rather than feeding their larvae, will seal them with all the food they will need to develop and then leave them to hatch. Social bees (including the honey bee and the bumblebee) had originated by about 40 million years ago. They live in hives that are constructed of two layers of six-sided cells made by workers. The hives are made of a mixture of beeswax, which is created by worker bees, and propolis, a form of plant resin they collect. Food in the form of honey and nectar is then stored in the cells of the hive.

The lives and hives of social bees are highly organized. There are three groups that live within them: workers, drones and queens. At the centre is the queen, who lays the eggs that reproduce the swarm. She also produces chemicals that guide the behaviour of the hive. Workers are females who have not sexually developed; they collect food to feed larvae in the form of pollen and nectar, as well as even collecting water in dry weather. They are also responsible for building, cleaning and protecting the hive, which they will even cool by beating their wings. From their salivary glands, workers also produce a substance called royal jelly, which is used to feed grubs for the first three days of their existence. When a queen dies, a new one is created by feeding it a diet exclusively of royal jelly. Finally, there are the drones – males whose only purpose is to mate with the queen. During the winter, when the bees feed on honey and pollen they have stored and cluster into a ball to conserve warmth, drones are usually expelled from the hive.

Humans have probably been eating honey since our earliest ancestors encountered a hive and realized the substance therein was both edible and sweet (certainly monkeys have been observed feeding on honey from hives in the wild). The first people to domesticate bees were the ancient Egyptians. They kept them in artificial hives – creating ones made of pottery as well as woven straw. They also used smoke to drive bees out of their hives so they could collect the honey and wax inside – a technique still used by beekeepers today. The Egyptians ate honey and stored it in sealed jars and also used it to embalm mummies. Over time, humans discovered the mild antiseptic properties of honey, and used it to treat burns and lacerations. It was widely used in cooking and to make alcoholic drinks like mead, as well as to preserve fruit. The most common species of bee used by humans is the western honey bee. Naturally occurring across Asia, Africa and Europe, it was one of the first to be domesticated, probably because of its versatility – it can collect pollen from a wide range of different plants (some bees have evolved to just feed on one type). By the nineteenth century, it had also been introduced to the Americas, Australia and New Zealand. Before the mass production of sugar and the replacement of candles by electric light, bees provided the main sources of sweetness and illumination for most humans.

Humans have worked to harness the power of bees by creating new breeds that can be more efficient. Unfortunately, this has led to one of the most feared bees: the Africanized killer bee. It is a hybrid of African and European subspecies, created to make a bee that could live in a tropical climate. Unfortunately, it was accidentally released in Brazil in 1957 when twenty-six swarms escaped quarantine. These bees flourished and steadily spread north, reaching Mexico during the 1980s and crossing the American border in 1990. They live in smaller colonies than many social bees, so can nest in enclosed spaces. The killer bee will react to threats more aggressively and violently than other breeds: it has been known to chase people over half a mile if disturbed, and has been responsible for killing over 1,000 people.

Bees remain vital to humans. Without them, many species of plants would breed less efficiently. Furthermore, crops pollinated naturally by bees may be of a higher quality. Despite their importance, bees across the world are threatened by habitat loss, pesticides and climate change. Unless this is reversed, the decline of bees will have serious consequences for both the agricultural economy and the environment.

COWS

Since they were domesticated over 10,000 years ago, cows have been one of the most valued animals, primarily because they provide meat and milk. They have many other uses. Their skins can be used to make leather, while their bones and hooves can be used to make gelatine (as well as ground down to make fertilizer). Rendered cow fat, known as tallow, makes a range of products including soap, candles and explosives. Cow dung is an effective form of manure, and when dried can be used as a fuel. Cows can also be used as draught animals, and before mechanization they played a major role in ploughing, hauling and even driving machinery. It is unsurprising then, that owning cows has been the most important marker of status and wealth in many societies. Furthermore, many religions venerate cows; particularly Hinduism, which views them as sacred representations of divine beneficence. As a result, many

Hindu rulers forbade the killing of cows and their slaughter still remains illegal in many Indian states today.

The aurochs was a species of wild cattle that once lived across Eurasia and North Africa. Slightly bigger than modern cows, they were fierce, fast and their horns could cause serious injuries. Despite this, their potential as a draught animal and a source of meat and milk meant they were domesticated. This occurred independently in two places: the Near East, the origin of the humpless taurine cattle that are now the most numerous subspecies, and the Indian subcontinent, the home of the zebu, distinguished by a fatty hump on its shoulders, which is most common in South Asia and Africa. Cows were able to adapt to a wide range of climates and habitats and became one of the most common farm animals. Part of the reason for the global success of the cow is their ability to produce food from grazing land that might otherwise be left unused for agriculture. Cows can live on just grass because they digest its tough fibres by chewing, regurgitating and rechewing it several times. It is then broken down by bacteria and other microorganisms that live in their four-chambered stomach. Meanwhile, aurochs numbers steadily declined and the last known one died in Poland in 1627.

There are now over 1.4 billion cows in the world, and their numbers are going up as a result of increased global demand for their meat and milk over the last six decades. This is linked to rising global standards of living, which mean that millions of people who once could not have afforded to eat meat regularly can now do so. To satisfy this demand, livestock farming has become increasingly intensive and millions of hectares have been converted to pasture.

Compared to growing plants, raising livestock on pasture is an inefficient use of land. In one year, 10,000 square metres (110,000 square feet) used for grazing cows will produce enough to feed just one person, while using the same area of land to grow potatoes will feed twenty-two. In their search for pasture, farmers have often destroyed forests. This is particularly pronounced in the Amazon, where ranchers cut down and burn thousands of square kilometres of rainforest every year. If this deforestation continues unabated, it will have increasingly disastrous environmental effects. This is because the trees of the Amazon absorb carbon, thus slowing climate change as well as producing one-fifth of the world's oxygen through photosynthesis. Cows are also contributing to climate change in another way. As a by-product of their digestion they produce a high amount of methane (95 per cent of which comes from burps), a harmful greenhouse gas that causes around 20 per cent of global warming. It may be possible to combat this by selectively breeding out the methane-producing microbes in the cow's digestive tract.

VACCINATION

Smallpox was once a global scourge, killing over one-third of those infected. In 1796, the English physician Edward Jenner (1749–1823) realized milkmaids who had contracted cowpox, a similar but milder disease, from cows may have immunity to smallpox. He then used material from a cowpox sore to create a smallpox immunization. 'Vaccination' (from the Latin for cow) led to the global eradication of smallpox by 1980, and the concept has been used to develop immunizations for other diseases.

Cattle farmers face thin profit margins, motivating them to maximize the productivity of their herds whenever possible. Selective breeding has created dairy cows that produce higher volumes of milk. Among cows raised for meat, the main aim of breeding is getting them to slaughter weight as quickly as possible. This is also achieved by diet; in many areas, particularly the United States, cows are often not raised on pasture but fed corn (and sometimes grains and soy), which is higher in starches and sugars than grass and causes them to gain weight faster, as does the common practice of administering growth hormones to them. Feeding cows a diet they are not naturally suited to often causes health problems, and they are routinely given antibiotics to combat any infections that arise. Taken together, these techniques mean cows can be made ready for slaughter at just fifteen months, and sold to consumers at cheaper prices.

There have been unintended costs in this quest to make cattle farming as efficient as possible. This was dramatically shown by the outbreak of bovine spongiform encephalopathy (BSE), commonly known as 'mad cow disease', in the United Kingdom in the 1980s. This fatal neurodegenerative disease was caused by feeding cows infected protein supplements made from carcasses and offal of other animals. If humans eat beef infected with BSE, it can cause a variant of Creutzfeldt–Jakob disease, a condition where the brain cells become damaged, leading to death in around one year. This incident showed the need for caution with new techniques in cattle farming; increasing efficiency and decreasing costs may come at a cost to public health, as well as the environment.

SILKWORMS

. . . .

The Yellow Emperor is a mythical figure said to have ruled China during the twenty-seventh century BC. Among the many achievements of his century-long reign were introducing boats, bows and writing. His wife Leizu was responsible for another great feature of Chinese culture: sericulture – the cultivation of silkworms to make silk. According to legend, while she was drinking tea a silkworm cocoon fell in her cup. She used the cocoon to make silk thread, which she then weaved in her loom. Struck by the fabric's strength and smoothness, she ordered mulberry trees be planted for silkworms to feed on, before teaching other women how to make silk.

Native to China, silkworms are caterpillars; moths and butterflies in their larval stage. They are now completely domesticated, and do not exist in the wild. Silkworms develop from eggs, which after seven to fourteen days of incubation hatch into 1-millimetre-long (0.04 inches) caterpillars. These feed on mulberry leaves, growing to 5 grams (0.2 ounces) in weight and 8 to 9 centimetres (around 3 inches) long in around thirty days. In preparation for turning into a moth, they wrap themselves in a cocoon made of a continuous strand of filaments, which they produce from two glands on the underside of their jaws. After three days in its cocoon, the caterpillar emerges as a silk moth.

Silkworms were first cultivated to make silk in China by the mid-third millennium BC. In the centuries after this time, silks began to be made using a similar process in India, but with different species of moths. The production of raw silk is a laborious process. Silkworms need to be kept at a constant temperature of 24 to 29 degrees Celsius (75 to 84 degrees Fahrenheit). This meant that fires in the rooms they were kept in had to be constantly stoked to ensure it did not grow too cold. After they hatch into silkworms, they are placed on trays along with mulberry leaves. They must not be allowed to break out of their cocoons because this would destroy the filaments. Instead, the cocoons are placed in hot, dry ovens or steamed, to kill the larva. Silk-workers then painstakingly unwind the filaments onto a spool. The strands are then spun into thread, which can be weaved into textiles. Silk is soft, dyes well and is strong but lightweight. Outputs are low. It takes 50,000 cocoons to make 1 kilogram (2.2 pounds) of thread. As a result, silk has always been a luxury product. Despite its expense, silk was much sought-after, and demand for the material helped create a trade network that linked Europe and Asia together.

The Han dynasty ruled China from 202 BC to AD 220. In around 130 BC, Emperor Wu of Han (157–87 BC) decided to open China to trade with areas to the west. This led to the creation of the 'Silk Road', a network of trade routes that started in Xi'an in Northwest China and stretched through Central Asia to the Mediterranean coast. It also included sections that extended to Arabia, Persia, the Indian subcontinent and South East Asia. As well as silk, goods such as tea, dyes, porcelain, spices, medicine, paper, gunpowder and jade were sent west, while horses, grapes, furs, skins, honey, precious metals and amber went east. Ideas travelled along the Silk Road, and it played a major role in spreading Buddhism and Christianity, but diseases were also carried along the route, and it was probably responsible for introducing plague to Europe.

Silk became incredibly fashionable among the Roman elite, prompting moralists to denounce it as decadent and immoral; there was even an imperial decree in the first century AD banning men from wearing it. In the long term, this did little to dent silk's popularity. For

Europeans, the main problem with silk was its eye-watering expense. The Chinese government ensured that the means of producing silk did not go west, by carefully searching trade caravans for silkworms (however, their techniques of silk-making were practised in other Asian countries – for example, in Korea by the first century BC and in Japan by the third century AD). This changed in the sixth century AD, when two monks brought silkworms to Constantinople, having managed to smuggle them inside their hollow bamboo canes. From Constantinople, silk-making eventually spread to many parts of Europe, and by the medieval period France and Italy were the two main European centres of its production. They remained so until the nineteenth century, when the European silk industry declined as a result of epidemics of diseases among their silkworms, and also due to imports from China and Japan, which had become cheaper since the Suez Canal opened in 1869.

Trade along the Silk Road remained highly significant for much of the medieval period. After the mid-fourteenth century, the collapse of the Mongol Empire led to political fragmentation in the areas it passed through. This disrupted traffic along the Silk Road, as there was no longer a strong central power keeping order. Warfare between the Ottoman Empire and Persia also proved damaging. By the mid-fifteenth century, the Silk Road, though it still existed in some places, was no longer the transcontinental network it had once been. European nations began to seek out a sea route to the East, which would allow them to trade directly with Asia. This would help lay the foundations of European colonialism and imperialism in the New World, and usher in a new era of globalization.

IMPERIAL PURPLE

Murex are a family of predatory sea snails that secrete a yellow fluid that after exposure to sunlight becomes a purple dye. It was popularized by the Phoenicians, who were trading it across the Mediterranean by 1200 BC. The dye was known as Tyrian purple because its main centre of production was Tyre, in modern-day Lebanon. The dye produced a vibrant colour that did not fade but was difficult and time-consuming to make, and so was an incredibly expensive luxury. Only wealthy elites could afford it, and in Rome it became associated with power and status.

Dromedary Camels

. . . .

Before the advent of motorized transport, camels were the backbone of long-distance trade in dry and arid regions that most other animals could not survive in, let alone be used to carry goods. Unlike the two-humped Bactrian camel, the dromedary has just one hump, which is used to store fat. This helps the dromedary to survive for up to one week without drinking. If they have access to water, they can rehydrate rapidly, by drinking over 100 litres (176 pints) in ten minutes. Dromedaries have many other features that help them work in the desert: they can survive on very little food and will forage plants other animals would not (for example, thorns). They also have three eyelids and two rows of long eyelashes that protect their eyes from the sand, and horny pads on their chest and knees that protect them from the heat when they lie down. Dromedaries' stamina, robustness and generally even temperament make them effective pack animals, and they can comfortably carry loads of 100 kilograms (220 pounds). They can also be used as draught animals or mounts, and provide food in the form of milk and meat. Dromedaries can sprint at speeds of 65 kilometres per hour (40 miles per hour) for short distances, making camel racing a popular sport in some places.

The dromedary was domesticated in Arabia between 3000 and 2000 BC (as a result it is also known as the Arabian camel). It was first introduced to Egypt in the ninth century BC and was commonly used across North Africa by the fourth century AD. Its most significant impact was in linking North and West Africa. Travel between these two regions required crossing the Sahara, which was dangerous and time-consuming. What made the risk and expense of crossing the Sahara worth it was the discovery in Europe of West Africa's rich deposits of gold. From the fourth century, trade caravans began crossing the Sahara, a journey of 1,000 kilometres (over 600 miles) that lasted up to three months. The Sahara was dominated by the Berber people of North

Africa, many of whom were nomadic herders. They had a rich knowledge of the region, and knew the location of the oases and wells that dotted the desert. In addition to gold, merchants travelling to West Africa sought to purchase enslaved people, ivory and ostrich feathers, among other things. The main import brought to West Africa was salt, which was in short supply in the region, as well as horses, perfumes and spices.

BACTRIAN CAMELS

The largest living camel species are the Bactrians, which are native to the Central Asian Steppe and were domesticated there as early as 4000 BC. Unlike dromedaries, they have two humps, and grow shaggy winter coats that allow them to withstand even very cold weather. Bactrian camels were one of the main pack animals used to carry goods on the Silk Road, and could carry loads of 200 kilograms (440 pounds) for 50 kilometres (30 miles) per day. The wild Bactrian camel is a related but separate species that lives in herds in northern China and southern Mongolia.

During the seventh and eighth centuries, the Umayyad Caliphate conquered North Africa; as a result, Islam became the majority religion there. During the invasion, the Arabs made use of the dromedary for scouting and mounted infantry and archers. In the following centuries, many Arab people migrated to North Africa, leading to Arabic become the main language of the region. Trans-Saharan trade, and dromedaries, were responsible for spreading Islam even further. The Berbers, who had largely converted to Islam, introduced the religion to many cities in West Africa. Its adherents included the rulers of the Mali Empire, which had become the dominant power in West Africa by the early thirteenth century, ruling 1.2 million square kilometres (around 500,000 square miles) of territory. Its most successful ruler was Musa I (*c*. 1280 – *c*. 1337), whose control of the gold trade made him one of the wealthiest people to have ever lived. When he made the pilgrimage to Mecca in 1324–5, he spent so lavishly in Cairo that the value of gold dropped by 20 per cent. The trans-Saharan trade also created cultural links, as many scholars, architects and craftsmen travelled to West Africa. As a result, the city of Timbuktu, founded by Berbers as a trading post in 1100, became one of the greatest centres of Islamic scholarship in the world.

The trans-Saharan trade began to decline in importance

from the later fifteenth century. This was because European nations, such as Portugal, Spain and England, established direct maritime routes to West Africa via the Atlantic. As a result, there was less need for goods to be carried across the Sahara, but dromedaries did remain important for local trade, particularly in more remote areas.

Dromedaries were not limited to just North Africa and Arabia; they were also incredibly important across the Middle East, the Indian subcontinent and, more recently, Australia. The European settlers who colonized Australia mostly clustered around the coastline, largely avoiding its vast, dry interior. Seeking to find some way to transport goods across it, from 1870 dromedaries began to be imported to Australia. Over the next fifty years, around 20,000 came, mostly from Arabia and the Indian subcontinent, joined by 2,000 handlers. These dromedaries helped to knit the country together, enabling long-distance trade. By the 1930s, the rise of the motor car had made them obsolete, and thousands were released into the outback. They thrived there, and by the early twenty-first century there was a population of around 1 million feral dromedaries spread out over an area of 3.3 million square kilometres (1.3 million square miles). Their presence has not always been welcome; they strip sparse grazing, destroy fences and break water pipes.

Consequently, the Australian government has followed a policy of mass culling, which has led to the population of feral dromedaries dropping to as low as 300,000. Dromedaries had shown they could easily survive in even the most uncompromising environments – it took the intervention of humans to reduce their numbers.

HERRINGS

Outside of the fishing industry, a piece of equipment called the power block is little known, but few inventions have had a more significant environmental and economic impact. Patented in 1953 by the Croatian-born American inventor Mario Puratić (1904–93), the power block is a mechanized winch that is used to haul fishing nets out of the water. Previously, this task had been labour-intensive and time-consuming, and easily disrupted by rough weather. Using the power block revolutionized fishing, making hauling nets quicker and easier, and possible even in poor weather. Combined with other innovations, like the use of sonar and synthetic nets, it allowed commercial fishing boats to go into deeper waters and land a greater catch than ever before. This included the herring, a species of bony, oily fish also known as the 'silver of the sea', for both its colour and the fortunes it could bring.

One of the most abundant fish species in the world, herrings are mostly found in the North Pacific and North Atlantic. They travel in schools of hundreds of thousands that are sometimes several kilometres across, mostly around coastlines and oceanic banks (areas where the sea is relatively shallower). They feed on the wide range of small marine organisms and animals that are collectively known as plankton. In turn, herrings are hunted by a wide range of predators, including cod, tuna, salmon, sharks, whales, seals and seabirds.

Herrings are migratory, spending the year moving from the open sea to their spawning grounds on the coast and back to the open sea. Herring eggs are about 1 millimetre (0.04 inches) in diameter; females deposit them on the seabed, releasing around 30,000 at a time. They hatch in around ten to fourteen days, although many of them will be eaten or washed ashore before then. There are several different groups or 'stocks' of herring, each of which have their own migratory pattern and spawning time and place. For reasons still not fully understood, their annual movements are often unpredictable. This means that sometimes a stock can seem to disappear from its usual area one year, or have a very low catch, and then reappear as usual the next year.

In the medieval and early modern period, consumption of fish was high because the Catholic Church demanded abstinence from meat during Lent and on other fast days. In Northern Europe, herring was one of the most popular fish. It was usually preserved by being salted, although it was also smoked, pickled, dried, cured and fermented. The trade in Baltic herring was particularly lucrative. In 1241, merchants from the coastal city of Lübeck, in modern-day northern Germany, formed an alliance with Hamburg, which had access to salt. This led to the Hanseatic League, a trading organization that grew to include around 200 towns and cites in Northern Europe. By the fourteenth century, the League dominated the Baltic economy, trading in not only salted herring but metals, grain, timber, textiles and furs. However, from the later fifteenth century, their power began to fade in the face of competition from other nations, and the League effectively ceased activities after 1669. Among the rising powers in the Baltic were the Dutch, who in 1415 launched the herring buss. This was a type of sailing ship specifically designed to trawl for herring. After the nets were hauled in, the herring catch was salted and barrelled immediately. Essentially, these were precursors to today's factory ships.

During the later nineteenth century, the British pioneered the use of steam-powered trawlers. These could travel faster and over greater distances, as well as being less vulnerable to bad weather conditions. They could also carry larger nets and more fish. By then, cold-smoked herrings, known as kippers, were a popular product, and distributed internationally. Due to increased demand and more effective trawling techniques, by the mid-twentieth century, when diesel-powered trawlers had become widespread, herring numbers were in decline and some stocks collapsed. This was particularly damaging for countries like Norway and Iceland, whose economies were traditionally highly reliant on fishing. Since then, conservation efforts and fishing quotas have led to a resurgence in herring numbers.

Although herring fishing is generally now sustainable, the same cannot be said for other species. In the aftermath of World War II, governments around the world subsidized their fishing industries, seeking to ensure their food supply. As a result, over the next four decades the annual world fishing catch quadrupled, peaking at 90 billion kilograms (90 million tons) in 1989. This rapid expansion also led to problems of bycatch, where animals like sharks, whales, dolphins and sea turtles are unintentionally caught in nets and killed. In particular, stocks of popular fish like cod, sea bass and tuna declined rapidly, leading to imbalances in the marine ecosystem. There were even fears that continuing to fish at these rates would lead to the collapse of global fisheries by 2048. In light of this, many countries moved to set limits to conserve their fisheries, but illegal poaching and quota-breaking remain problematic. Greater efforts are required for fishing to remain sustainable into the twenty-first century and beyond.

THE COD WARS

Iceland and the United Kingdom have engaged in three armed stand-offs over fishing rights – the 'Cod Wars'. They occurred in 1958–61, 1972–3 and 1975–6, caused by Iceland's progressive extension of its national waters to secure its fishing stocks. On each occasion, British trawlers continued to operate in Icelandic waters. The Royal Navy was sent in to protect them from Icelandic patrol vessels. Despite incidents of ramming, net-cutting and firing of shots over bows, there was no escalation of hostilities. The Cod Wars ended when Iceland threatened to leave NATO, which would have had severe geopolitical implications. Consequently, the United Kingdom accepted Iceland's extension of its territorial waters to 370 kilometres (230 miles) from its coast.

BEAVERS

. . . .

Apart from humans, the animal that most changes the environment to suit its purposes is the beaver. There are two extant species of this large, semi-aquatic rodent: the North American beaver and the Eurasian beaver. The backbone of their diet is cambium, the moist layer of plant tissue underneath a tree's bark, but they also eat buds, leaves and twigs. Both species live in streams, rivers, marshes and ponds, and on lake shorelines. They construct their homes, which are called 'lodges', by piling up logs, branches and mud in the water to build a dome-like structure with two underwater entrances that are around 4 metres (13 feet) high and up to 12 metres (40 feet) across. The interior houses a breeding pair and their children and includes a cache of food for the winter months. To deter predators, beavers build dams around their lodges, which makes the surrounding water deeper. The largest known example was seen in Alberta, Canada, and was 800 metres (875 yards) long. Beavers even dig 'canals' to float trees they have felled to their lodges and dams.

As the beaver's lifestyle is dependent on being able to gnaw through wood, they have chisel-shaped incisors whose outer layer is made of iron. Beavers can spend up to fifteen minutes underwater, and have evolved into strong swimmers, using their tail as a rudder, with webbed hind feet, a membrane that protects their eyes, and folds of skin that close over their nostrils and ears. It is the beaver's fur that has made it so desired by humans; it is thick, sleek and water-repellent. The trade in their pelts would help shape North American history, motivating European powers to expand further into the region and contributing to imperial rivalry.

During the fifteenth and sixteenth centuries, Western Europe's main source of beaver pelts was from Russia and northern Scandinavia (their range extended across much of Eurasia from Britain to Central Asia, but over-hunting had greatly reduced their numbers in many areas). As the fur was so dense, it made very high-quality felt that was used to make hats. Although expensive, beaver hats were highly valued because they were water-repellant and held their shape well. It was also claimed that the oils in the pelts could improve the wearer's memory and build their intelligence. Beavers also provided another valuable commodity, castoreum, which is a thick liquid substance they secrete to mark territory. It was highly valued as an ingredient in perfumes, medicines and even used as a food flavouring. Consumer demand greatly reduced the numbers of the Eurasian beaver, driving it to extinction by the early seventeenth century. However, there was another source of beaver pelts: North America.

Before the arrival of Europeans, there were around 200 million beavers in North America, ranging as far south as Mexico, but most concentrated in modern-day sub-arctic Canada, Alaska and the Great Lakes region. European traders all sought to take advantage of the abundance of beavers, sending out trappers as well as hiring indigenous guides. They also established trading posts where they would purchase beaver pelts from Native American and First Nations peoples in exchange for goods like guns and textiles. The struggle for preferential access to trade with Europeans contributed to the 'Beaver Wars', a series of conflicts lasting from the early seventeenth century to 1701 between the Iroquois, a confederacy of tribes generally supported by the Dutch and English, and the Algonquins, allies of France. Thanks to the supply from North America, the European beaver-hat-making industry, which was largely centred in England, France and Russia, flourished. The flood of beaver pelts reduced prices, and many of the hats were re-exported back across the Atlantic.

By the early eighteenth century, the two main colonial powers in North America were England and France. Their colonists frequently clashed, often over access to hunting grounds, and open warfare broke out in 1754. This was folded into the wider Seven Years' War, which was the first global conflict and lasted from 1756 to 1763. In North America, it saw Britain defeat the French, forcing them to cede their possessions there (with the exception of two small islands off the coast of Newfoundland). This allowed British traders to dominate the beaver trade. Fortunately for the North American beaver, from the mid-nineteenth century, silk replaced felt as the most fashionable material to make hats with. This probably helped to save the North American beaver from extinction.

ARGENTINIAN BEAVERS

In 1946, the Argentinian government introduced beavers to the region of Tierra del Fuego, which is in the southernmost part of the country. They hoped their pelts would become a valuable commodity, but a drop in global demand for animal fur meant this never transpired. The beavers, lacking natural predators, flourished. Their activities rerouted rivers and damaged local trees and grassland, and they chewed through cables, disrupting energy supply and communications. There are now 70,000 to 110,000 beavers spread over an area of 70,000 square kilometres (27,000 square miles), and they have spread into neighbouring Chile.

Even though their pelts were no longer in high demand, decades of hunting, exacerbated by habitat loss, meant that by 1900 there were perhaps as few as 100,000 North American beavers left. Since then, conservation efforts have increased their numbers to around 10 million. Populations of Eurasian beavers are less healthy; at the beginning of the twentieth century, as few as 1,200 remained, but since then their numbers have increased to over 600,000 and there have even been successful reintroductions in some areas, such as Mongolia, Britain and Sweden. Healthy beaver populations are vital because their dams help extend wetland, creating habitats for waterfowl and fish. They also help to filter out pollution and sediment in water, reduce erosion and help reduce the severity of forest fires by acting as firebreaks. For all that its pelt was once treasured, the true value of the beaver is in maintaining healthy ecosystems.

AMERICAN BISON

On 9 May 2016, the American bison was officially named the national mammal of the United States. Over five centuries ago, there were between 30 and 60 million of these grazing bovines in the interior of the North American continent. They lived in the highest densities on the Great Plains, an expanse of flat land between the Mississippi River and the Rocky Mountains in modern-day Canada and the United States.

The American bison evolved from the now-extinct steppe bison, which originated in South Asia and migrated to the Americas via the Bering land bridge between 300,000 and 130,000 years ago. The American bison reaches heights of 2 metres (over 6 feet) at the shoulder and weights of 900 kilograms (2,000 pounds), but the steppe bison was even larger and had longer horns and two humps instead of one.

Between 40,000 and 15,000 years ago, humans migrated to the Americas using the Bering land bridge, settling across the continent. Some were the ancestors of the indigenous peoples of the United States and Canada, known collectively as Native Americans and First Nations, respectively. The bison was central to the way of life of those who lived on the Great Plains. It provided them with meat, and the hide was used to make shoes, robes and coverings for tipis. Its teeth, sinews and horns were used to make tools, weapons and jewellery, while even its rough, bristly tongue was used as a comb.

The arrival of Europeans in North America violently destabilized its ecosystem as well as the way of life of its indigenous peoples. Their populations were decimated by new diseases and violence, and their lands were colonized. Following the American victory in their war of independence from the British in 1783, the United States steadily expanded westward. This brought Europeans into closer contact with the bison, which they often called 'buffalo', because of its resemblance to another group of bovines that lives in sub-Saharan Africa and South East Asia. From the later eighteenth century, numbers of bison began to decline. They had disappeared from east of the Mississippi River by the early nineteenth century and from west of the Rocky Mountains by 1840, leaving the only remaining herds on the Great Plains. There, they lost grazing land to farms and ranches that were established in its usual habitat. In addition, bison caught diseases from livestock, most seriously brucellosis and tuberculosis.

The main cause of the falling bison population was hunting. Bison were sought-after for their hides, which were used to make coats and blankets. The only other parts of the body European hunters tended to be interested in were the hump and tongue, which were eaten. The rest of the carcass was left to rot. By the mid-nineteenth century, hunters armed with guns were flocking to the Great Plains, drawn by the profits to be made from the bison. In addition, Native Americans who had been dispossessed of their ancestral lands on the Eastern Seaboard were forcibly resettled on the Great Plains, creating tension with the existing indigenous population and putting greater pressure on resources.

On 17 September 1851, the American government signed the Treaty of Fort Laramie with representatives of several Native American tribes. This, and dozens of other similar agreements, set aside land for the Native Americans. These treaties would largely be reneged on. Europeans settled on Native American land, and also mined there if deposits of precious metals were discovered. The arrival of the railway was also transformative; it tied together the East and West Coast of the United States, indiscriminately cutting through Native American land. Symbolic of this was the completion of the Union Pacific Railroad, the first-ever transcontinental line, in 1869. Bison were killed by the thousand to feed the workers who built it.

During the 1860s, tensions increased between Native Americans of the Great Plains and settlers, leading to violent skirmishes. In response, the American government moved towards a policy of forcing the Native American population into reservations – any tribes who refused were deemed 'hostile' and subjected to warfare. Conflict between Native Americans and government forces would continue until the early twentieth century, and culminate in their forced resettlement in reservations. One of the main methods of weakening Native American resistance was to target the bison. There was ample public enthusiasm for killing bison; in addition to commercial hunters, social elites would travel to the Great Plains to shoot them for 'sport' from the comfort of trains. Even though it was illegal, the US Army turned a blind eye to people who crossed into reservations to hunt bison. Some states passed local laws to protect bison, but they were widely ignored and in 1874, after Congress passed a bill that limited bison hunting, President Ulysses S. Grant (1822–85) refused to sign it into law. The first national legislation that protected the bison was passed in Canada in 1877, but it was repealed the next year.

EUROPEAN BISON

As well as crossing into North America, the steppe bison migrated west, where they interbred with the aurochs. This led to the evolution of the European bison, which was larger and longer-legged than the American bison. European bison once lived in woodland across the continent but by the 1920s had been hunted into extinction in the wild. They were reintroduced using specimens kept in zoos, and the first were released into Białowieża Forest in north-eastern Poland. There are now around 6,000 wild European bison, living in Poland, Belarus, Lithuania, Russia and Ukraine.

By 1889, there were fewer than 1,000 wild bison left in North America. This sparked a belated conservation effort that saw natural preserves permanently set aside for them and laws that protected them from hunters and poachers. In addition, bison herds that had been bred on ranches were released into the wild. There are now 20,000 wild bison in the United States and 10,000 in Canada; these numbers are enough to secure their long-term future, but represent only a small fraction of their historical population.

BLUE WHALES

In 1864, the *Spes et Fides* was launched; its owner and designer was the Norwegian Svend Foyn (1809–94). The ship was 29 metres (95 feet) long and the first steam-powered whaling ship (although it also had sails to supplement its engine). It had a top speed of 13 kilometres per hour (8 miles per hour), a powered winch to haul in whale carcasses, and deck-mounted guns that could fire explosive harpoons. These innovations would eventually make its design the industry standard for the next six decades. They allowed whaling ships to venture into colder, more remote waters and pursue larger prey, including the blue whale.

Blue whales are the largest animal to have ever lived, reaching lengths of 30 metres (100 feet) and weighing 180,000 kilograms (nearly 180 tons). Their hearts can weigh up to 700 kilograms (over 1,500 pounds), and their arteries are big enough for a child to crawl through. Blue whales are found in every ocean, spending their spring and summer in colder waters and migrating to the equator in winter for breeding season. As well as being the largest animal, blue whales are also one of the loudest – their 'song' (which helps them communicate and navigate) can be detected at distances of over 1,500 kilometres (over 900 miles) and reaches volumes of over 180 decibels, louder than a jet launching. However, the sounds it makes are too low in frequency for humans to hear them.

Unlike the toothed whales, which include species like the sperm whale, narwhal and orca, and which hunt for fish, squid and even seals, blue whales feed mostly on tiny crustaceans called krill. They do this by swallowing water and forcing it out of their mouths. The krill are trapped by 1-metre-long (3 feet) plates of baleen, which are thick bristles made of keratin inside their mouths, and then swallowed. There are fourteen other species of baleen whale, including the humpback, gray and fin whale.

Humans have been hunting whales for at least 5,000 years. The first to do so were probably the Inuit, the indigenous peoples of the Arctic, who come from modern-day Alaska, northern Canada and Greenland (whaling was also practised in ancient Japan and Korea). Using boats and harpoons tied to ropes, they would hunt smaller whales that could be beached and larger ones only if they swam into bays. For the Inuit, whales are, and continue to be, an important source of food, as their skin, blubber and internal organs are a rich source of protein, fat, vitamins and minerals. Furthermore, whale bones and teeth can be used to make tools and weapons, while their sinews could make ropes and baleen could be made into baskets and mats.

The commercial hunting of whales began in medieval Europe. Its first major practitioners were the Basques, who were sending out whaling vessels by the eleventh century AD. By the seventeenth century, the English, Dutch and Norwegians had established their own whaling industries, as had European colonists in North America. Their ships initially operated mainly in the North Atlantic, but from the eighteenth century expanded operations into the Pacific and Indian oceans. They launched smaller boats that could be rowed close enough to whales to harpoon them. If the hunt was successful, the whale would be towed back to the main ship to be processed.

The most important part of the whale's body was its blubber, which while still on board ships was rendered into oil and stored in casks. It was then sold to be used as a lubricant and in lighting. Baleen also had a wide range of uses, including roofing, carriage springs, ribs of corsets and hoops for skirts. Whale meat, though eaten in some places, tended not to be traded commercially because it spoiled quickly. The Industrial Revolution, which started in Britain in the later eighteenth century and then spread into Western Europe and North America, created great demand for whale oil. Up to the mid-nineteenth century, blue whales tended not to be prized by whaling captains. This was because they were too big to butcher quickly and would often sink before they could be towed back to the ship. In addition, because they could swim at speeds of up to 50 kilometres per hour (30 miles per hour) if fleeing danger, they were too fast for whaling ships to pursue.

By the early twentieth century, the blue whale's sheer bulk no longer protected it from whaling ships. Adopting techniques pioneered by Norwegians, the whaling industry began to venture into the colder waters of the Antarctic and South Atlantic, and made use of spotter aircraft and radios to locate targets. Factory ships efficiently processed whales into oil at sea. The whole carcass was used; even the bones were boiled up with meat to make low-grade oil, and any residue that remained was ground down to make fertilizer or animal feed. Whale oil was in high demand for use in making soap and margarine, and was also used to make glycerine, a component of explosives. In addition, the advent of refrigerator ships meant that whale meat could be preserved at sea long enough to be sold. As a result, from 1900 to the 1960s, over 360,000 blue whales were killed.

The international whaling industry peaked in 1961, with a total of 66,000 blue whales killed. By then, it was clear that their numbers were in rapid decline, and there was increasing clamour for them to be protected. The International Whaling Commission, established in 1946 to conserve whale stocks and monitor the industry, began to enforce stricter quotas and controls. In 1966, the hunting of blue whales was completely banned, and an international moratorium on all commercial whaling came into force in 1986. As a result, whale numbers have generally increased, although they still face illegal hunting, climate change, collisions with ships, entanglement in nets and sound pollution caused by increased human marine activity. There are now between 10,000 and 25,000 blue whales worldwide, and, although this is no more than one-tenth of their population a century ago, it does mean the world's largest animal is no longer in critical danger of extinction.

CONCLUSION

·⁛·

A Short History of the World in 50 Animals shows that it is not only humans who can tell a story about how the world has changed. Indeed, in comparison to the likes of sharks and birds, humans are an incredibly recent addition to the planet, making an understanding of other animals a vital way to appreciate change in the very long term. However, the history of the animal world also allows a new perspective on humanity, and how it has viewed, been shaped by and used other animals. In particular, this book shows how humans have radically changed the planet. Ultimately, mastery, control and even exploitation of other animals has been fundamental to *Homo sapiens* becoming the most dominant form of life. Without other animals, humans would not have been able to flourish as they did – they have provided nutrition, shelter, transport, clothing and medicine, among numerous other things. Indeed, as the story of Laika the Dog shows, animals have also helped humans as they move to explore beyond the confines of Earth.

This harnessing of the natural world to the benefit of humans comes at a peril, both to ourselves and other animals. As humans have thrived and spread out across every continent, they have left an indelible and perhaps irreversible footprint. The movement of humans around the world has also, in many respects, concurrently been a movement of other animals, some of which have spread disease and caused countless deaths. The spread of humans has also led to the extinction of some animals, such as the dodo and passenger pigeon, which have suffered from both loss of natural habitat and the introduction of invasive species that preyed on them. In the long term, a more sustainable relationship between humans and animals demands a greater understanding and consideration of how they have, and will, impact on each other, as well as the wider environment.

ACKNOWLEDGEMENTS

Thank you, once again, to the wonderful team at Michael O'Mara Books – this book could not have happened without them. In particular, special thanks to my editor, Gabriella Nemeth, for her encouragement, expertise and advice, as well as David Inglesfield for copy-editing and Aubrey Smith for the illustrations. Furthermore, thank you to my students and teaching colleagues, past and present, for their insights, enthusiasm and historical discussions. Finally, thank you to everyone at Mayhew, the animal welfare charity, for all their amazing work and advocacy on behalf of cats, dogs and communities (as well as rescuing our feline friend, Roman the Cat).

Select Bibliography

Birkhead, T.R., *The Wisdom of Birds: An Illustrated History of Ornithology*, Bloomsbury, 2011

Coyne, J.A., *Why Evolution Is True*, Oxford University Press, 2010

Field, J.F., *A Short History of the World in 50 Places*, Michael O'Mara Books, 2020

Francis, R.C., *Domesticated: Evolution in a Man-Made World*, W.W. Norton, 2015

Kemmerer, L., *Animals and World Religions*, Oxford University Press, 2011

Leeming, D., *The Oxford Companion to World Mythology*, Oxford University Press, 2009

Prothero, D.R., *Evolution: What the Fossils Say and Why It Matters*, Columbia University Press, 2007

Resh, V.H., and Cardé, R.T. (eds), *Encyclopedia of Insects*, Academic Press, 2009

Roberts, C., *The Unnatural History of the Sea*, Island Press, 2009

Vitt, L.J., and Caldwell, J.P., *Herpetology: An Introductory Biology of Amphibians and Reptiles*, Academic Press, 2013

Weishampel, D.B., Dodson, P., and Osmolska, H. (eds), *The Dinosauria*, University of California Press, 2007

Wilson, E.O., *The Diversity of Life*, Penguin, 2001

INDEX